CGP GEOGRAPHY RESOURCES

GCSE GEOGRAPHY

The Essential Revision Guide (OCR C)

This book perfectly covers the human and physical geography content for the OCR Examining Board, specification C.

The information is explained fully, and written concisely so that each topic can be displayed on a single page.

Contents

Published by CGP

Editors:
Kate Houghton
Becky May
Rachel Selway

Contributors:
Sheila Ambury, Rosalind Browning, Paul Boulton, Martin Chester, Simon Cook,
Chris Dennett, Leigh Edwards, Catherine Graley, Dominic Hall, Tim Major,
Barbara Melbourne, David Rourke, Emma Singleton, James Paul Wallis.

With thanks to Edward Robinson and Eileen Worthington for proofreading.

Types of Rock

Rocks are classed as igneous, sedimentary or metamorphic, depending on how they were formed.

Igneous Rocks are formed from *Magma*

Extrusive igneous rocks are formed when magma spills out on to the surface as lava and cools there (e.g. volcanic rocks). They have a fine texture (e.g. basalt). When the magma cools very slowly, large hexagonal columns form.

<table>
<tr><td>

KEY TERMS

Magma is hot, molten rock, found inside the Earth, in the **mantle** — the area beneath the Earth's top layer (the **crust**).

</td></tr>
</table>

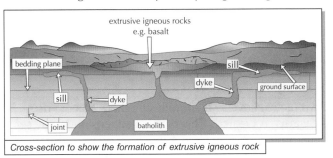

Cross-section to show the formation of extrusive igneous rock

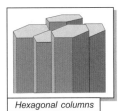

Hexagonal columns

Intrusive igneous rocks like granite occur when magma cools very slowly before reaching the surface. They have a coarse texture and form features like batholiths and tors. If magma flows along rock openings before cooling it forms sills and dykes made of another igneous rock, dolerite.

Tors are granite structures that have been worn down to leave large square blocks.

EXAMPLES

Igneous Rocks	
Type	Example
Extrusive (Hexagonal columns)	Giant's Causeway in Northern Ireland
Intrusive (Tors)	The tors on Dartmoor

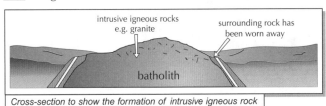

Cross-section to show the formation of intrusive igneous rock

Tors

Sedimentary Rocks are formed from *Particles*

Sandstones, shales and clays are made from tiny particles of sand or clay eroded from past landscapes by wind or water and deposited in layers, for example in the sea. Later they're uplifted to a position above sea-level. These layers are beds or strata — separated by bedding planes.

Carboniferous limestone and chalk are formed from the remains of tiny shells and micro-skeletons. They're made of calcium carbonate and react with dilute hydrochloric acid.

Coal is made from carbonaceous (carbon rich) remains of tropical plants.

EXAM TIP

It's easy to get all the different types of rock mixed up. Make a list of all the new words with their definitions, and learn them separately.

Metamorphic Rocks are formed by *Heat* or *Pressure*

'Metamorphic' just means 'changed form'. Igneous or sedimentary rocks can be transformed during volcanic activity or earth movements. The chemical composition is the same but the new rocks are harder, more compact and crystalline.

Sandstone		Quartzite		Limestone		Marble
Clays		Slate		Granite		Gneiss

Landscapes Shaped by Tectonics

The Earth's crust is made of huge floating 'tectonic plates'. These plates are constantly moving, helping to form many of the landscapes we know.

The Earth's Crust is Divided up into <u>Tectonic Plates</u>

Tectonic plates 'float' or move very slowly (a few mm per year) on the molten material of the <u>mantle</u> (the liquid insides of the Earth). This movement is caused by <u>convection currents</u> (see page 34) in the mantle. Plates meet at <u>plate boundaries</u> or <u>margins</u>. Plate movements create <u>landforms</u> — <u>volcanoes</u> and <u>fold mountain ranges</u> are found at plate margins.

There are <u>Three</u> Types of Plate Margin

<u>Divergent margins:</u>

EXAMPLES

Iceland and Hawaii are examples of volcanic islands formed at divergent margins.

At tensional margins, two plates move <u>away</u> from each other. Magma rises from the mantle and <u>new crust</u> is created. This mostly happens under the sea. <u>Volcanoes</u> are also common under the sea at tensional boundaries. They can become so big that they eventually form new <u>islands</u>.

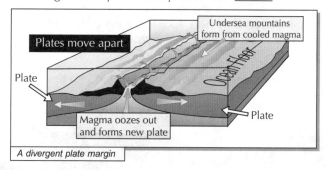

A divergent plate margin

<u>Convergent margins:</u>

Two plates move <u>towards</u> each other and crust is destroyed.
<u>Fold mountains</u>, <u>earthquakes</u> and <u>volcanoes</u> are common.

EXAMPLES

Plate Margins	Example
Divergent	Mid-Atlantic Ridge
Convergent	West coast of South America
Transform	San Andreas Fault (San Francisco)

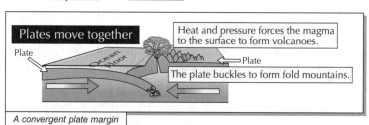

A convergent plate margin

<u>Transform margins:</u>

Plates move <u>sideways</u> against each other and material is neither gained nor lost. Volcanoes are rare at these margins, but <u>earthquakes</u> are common as <u>pressure</u> builds up and is released when the plates jerk past each other. Transform margins have less ability to shape the landscape than the other types of margin, but land can still become <u>ridged</u> and <u>crumpled</u>.

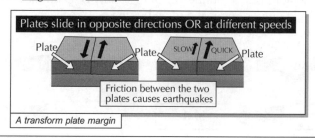

A transform plate margin

Weathering

Weathering is the breakdown of rocks by physical, chemical or biological processes — it takes place on site, so there is no movement involved.

Physical Weathering _Breaks Down_ Rock Surfaces

Freeze-thaw action in temperate climates:

In the British Isles, temperatures are around 0° C on many winter nights. Water gets trapped in cracks in the rock. It expands when it freezes, pressurising the rock sides. During the day, the water melts and contracts, releasing pressure on the rock cracks.

This alternating expansion and contraction weakens the rock and pieces break off, a process called frost shattering. It produces scree at the foot of steep slopes and blockfields (big jagged rocks lying about) on gentle ones.

EXAMPLE

The slopes around Wast Water in the Lake District are famous for their scree slopes.

Frost shattering

Onion-skin weathering in hot desert climates:

Hot desert areas have a big daily temperature range (typically 35° C in the day, 10° C at night). Each day, surface layers of rock heat up and expand. At night the cold makes them contract — this causes thin layers to peel off.

  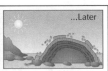

Onion skin weathering

Biological Weathering needs _Plant Roots_ or _Decay_

Plant roots can grow down through cracks in rock surfaces and push them apart, loosening fragments. Decaying plants and animal remains make acids which eat away at the rocks below.

Chemical Weathering Involves _Reactions_ on the Rock

Limestone areas are weathered when limestone reacts with rainwater (a weak carbonic acid). When it rains, the rock is dissolved along weaknesses like joints and bedding planes, forming solution features (e.g. caves, swallow holes and the clints and grykes of limestone pavements). Water droplets leave the dissolved rock behind on cave roofs and floors to form stalactites and stalagmites.

Granite areas react chemically, rotting down to form kaolin (china clay).

EXAMPLES

The Malham area in North Yorkshire is a limestone area. It has caves with impressive stalactites and stalagmites.

Cornwall is a granite area, parts of which have been mined for china clay.

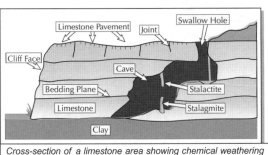

Cross-section of a limestone area showing chemical weathering

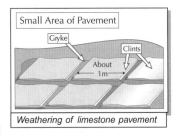

Weathering of limestone pavement

Rivers and Valleys

The different stages of a river's course each have their own characteristics.

Rivers Flow in Linear Features called <u>Valleys</u>

A <u>river</u> flows from an <u>upland source</u> to the <u>mouth</u> where it enters the sea. The river channel <u>widens</u> as it follows its course to the sea, and the <u>amount</u> of water it carries (its <u>discharge</u>) increases as <u>other</u> streams and rivers <u>join it</u>.

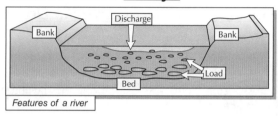
Features of a river

High <u>velocity</u> (the speed of flow in one direction) results in high <u>energy</u> — e.g. during floods or when the river's gradient is steep. Rivers with lots of energy wear away the <u>channel bed</u> and <u>banks</u>, producing the <u>load</u> — sand and stones. When a river has little energy, the load is <u>deposited</u> on the <u>bed</u> and <u>banks</u>.

A Valley <u>Cross Profile</u> has Three Stages

<u>UPPER</u>: near the source it is V-shaped — it has a <u>narrow floor</u> and <u>steep sides</u>.
<u>MIDDLE</u>: lower down the river, the <u>floor</u> is <u>wider</u> and <u>sides</u> are more <u>gently sloping</u>.
<u>LOWER</u>: near to the sea, the river has a <u>wide floor</u> and <u>gentle sides</u>.

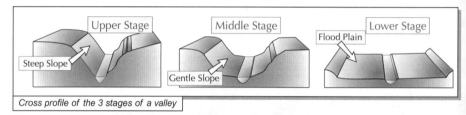
Cross profile of the 3 stages of a valley

A River's <u>Long Profile</u> Varies as it Moves Downstream

In the <u>upper</u> stage, the river's gradient is quite <u>steep</u>.

In the <u>middle</u> stage it's <u>more gentle</u>.

In the <u>lower</u> stage it's <u>very gentle</u> and almost <u>flat</u>.

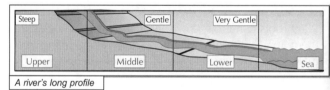
A river's long profile

<u>Erosion</u> is When the River Wears Land Away

Rivers erode in four main ways, called <u>erosion processes</u>:

<u>Corrasion</u> or <u>abrasion</u> is when large pieces of <u>bedload</u> material wear away the riverbed and banks — e.g. in floods. If material collects in a dip, it swirls around, forming a <u>pothole</u>.

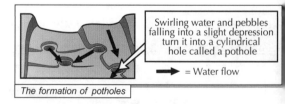
Swirling water and pebbles falling into a slight depression turn it into a cylindrical hole called a pothole
➡ = Water flow
The formation of potholes

<u>Attrition</u> means rocks being transported are <u>eroded</u>. <u>Sediment particles</u> knock against the bed or each other and <u>break apart</u>, becoming smaller and more round.

<u>Hydraulic action</u> is when the <u>force</u> of the water wears away at softer rocks such as clay. It can also <u>weaken</u> rocks along bedding planes and joints.

<u>Solution</u> or <u>corrosion</u> is when chalk and limestone <u>dissolve</u> in water.

SUMMARY

River cross profile		
Stage	Floor	Sides
Upper	Narrow	Steep
Middle	Wide	Gently sloping
Lower	Very wide	Gentle

KEY TERM

<u>Bedload</u> — rocks plucked from river bed and banks and carried along at the bottom of the river.

SUMMARY

Four types of erosion:
- **corrasion**
- **attrition**
- **hydraulic action**
- **solution**

Erosion, Transportation & Deposition

The ways that a river shapes the landscape can be grouped into three categories
— erosion (removing), transportation (moving) and deposition (leaving behind).

River Erosion is <u>Headward</u>, <u>Vertical</u> or <u>Lateral</u>

<u>Headward erosion</u> is when the furthest point
upstream, the <u>valley head</u>, is worn away by
<u>rainwash</u>, <u>undercutting</u> (see page 6) or <u>soil creep</u>
(the slow movement of soil downhill over time).

<u>Vertical erosion</u> deepens the valley as
the <u>water force grows</u> — common in the
<u>upper stage</u> when the gradient is steep.

<u>Lateral erosion</u> widens the valley, combined
with <u>weathering</u> of the sides — it's common
in <u>middle</u> and <u>lower</u> stage valleys.

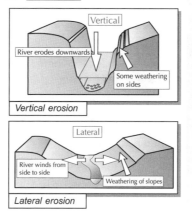

Vertical
River erodes downwards
Some weathering on sides
Vertical erosion

Lateral
River winds from side to side
Weathering of slopes
Lateral erosion

SUMMARY

River Erosion	
Type	**Description**
Headward Erosion	Wears away the valley head
Vertical Erosion	Deepens the valley
Lateral Erosion	Widens the valley

<u>Transportation</u> is the Movement of Eroded Material

A river transports its load downstream in four ways:

- <u>Suspension</u> is when fine silt and clay material is <u>carried</u> along in the water.

- <u>Saltation</u> is when small sand-sized particles are <u>bounced</u> along the <u>riverbed</u>.

- <u>Traction</u> — <u>larger</u> materials like boulders are <u>dragged</u> along the bed.

- <u>Solution</u> is when eroded material <u>dissolved</u> in the water is <u>carried away</u>.

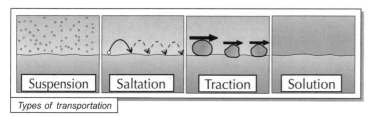

| Suspension | Saltation | Traction | Solution |

Types of transportation

<u>Deposition</u> is When a River Dumps its Load

Material is deposited where the flow of the river is slower

Deposition

It can happen when the <u>velocity</u> is
<u>lower</u> than normal and the river
can't move as much material.

It also happens when a river's <u>load</u> is
<u>increased</u> — e.g. after a landslide.

<u>Deposition</u> can form <u>deltas</u>
where rivers enter a <u>sea</u> or <u>lake</u>
(see page 7).

EXAMPLE

**The large natural levees
(raised river banks — see
p. 7) on the Mississippi
River are a good example
of depositional river
features.**

There are <u>Four Stages</u> of Deposition

- <u>Large material</u> carried by the river is <u>deposited</u> in the <u>higher reaches</u>.

- <u>Gravel, sand and silt</u> carried as bedload or in suspension
  are laid down in the <u>lower reaches</u>.

- Fine particles of <u>suspended silt</u> and <u>clay</u> are laid down in <u>estuaries</u> and <u>deltas</u>.

- <u>Dissolved load</u> is <u>not</u> deposited, but stays in solution and is carried out to sea.

River Features of the Upper Stage

Many of the more notable and dramatic river features are found at the upper stage.

Interlocking Spurs are Caused by Erosion

In its upper stage the river erodes vertically rather than laterally.

Interlocking spurs are ridges produced when a river in the upper stage twists and turns round obstacles of hard rock along its downward pathway.

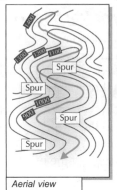

Aerial view

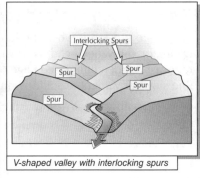

V-shaped valley with interlocking spurs

These ridges interlock with one another like the teeth of a zip fastener.

Waterfalls are Found at Steep Parts of the River Bed

A layer of hard rock won't erode very easily so when the river reaches it, any softer rocks on the downstream side are eroded more quickly. This means the river bed gets steeper where it crosses the hard rocks and a waterfall forms.

Waterfalls can form when the hard rock is horizontal, vertical or dips upstream (rock slopes down as you go upstream). At the foot of the waterfall the water wears away the softer rock to form a plunge pool.

As the waterfall retreats and eats its way upstream, a recessional gorge is formed.

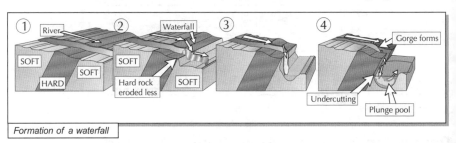

Formation of a waterfall

Rapids are a Series of Little Waterfalls

Rapids are found where there are alternate bands of hard and soft rock:

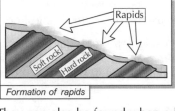

Formation of rapids

They can also be found when a hard rock layer dips downstream:

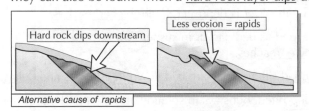

Alternative cause of rapids

River Features of Middle & Lower Stages

Middle and lower stage river features are often more temporary and changeable than upper stage features.

The Middle and Lower Stages have <u>Meanders</u>

The river now has a <u>large discharge</u>, <u>gentle gradient</u> and <u>lateral erosion</u>. It develops a more winding pathway with <u>large bends</u> — these bends are called <u>meanders</u>.

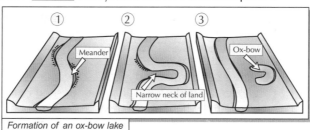

Aerial view — Point Bar, River Cliff, = Direction of strongest current. **Cross-section** — River Cliff, Slip-off slope, Point Bar, Strong current deep channel, Weaker current shallow channel.

Formation of meanders

The river twists — over time the course of the meander migrates <u>downstream</u>. The current is <u>fastest</u> on the <u>outside</u> of the meander curve, causing greater erosion here, so the channel becomes deeper. On the inside, the slower current causes deposition, making this area more shallow.

<u>River cliffs</u> are found on the meander's <u>outer edge</u> where the river causes more erosion. <u>Point bars</u> are on the <u>inner edge</u> where sandy material is <u>deposited</u> by the slower-moving river — above river level they're <u>slip-off slopes</u>.

<u>Ox-Bow Lakes</u> are Formed from Wide Meander Loops

<u>Meander loops</u> can become so <u>sinuous</u> (wavy) that the river's easiest path is straight across, so it breaks through the narrow <u>neck of land</u> in between.

The <u>outer part</u> of the loop is left <u>isolated</u> from the river as an <u>ox-bow lake</u>.

① Meander ② Narrow neck of land ③ Ox-bow

Formation of an ox-bow lake

FACT

Large rivers like the Amazon have many large meanders and ox-bow lakes. They are often short-term features — ox-bow lakes are gradually taken over by plants, become marshes and dry up.

The Lower Stage has Several <u>Important Features</u>

The river now has its greatest discharge and mass — it has a really big cross-sectional area.

- <u>Alluvium</u> is <u>all material</u> deposited by a river. It's usually very <u>fertile</u>.

- The <u>flood plain</u> is the <u>wide valley floor</u> which the river regularly floods. It's <u>flat</u> and covered by alluvium, making it <u>good farmland</u>.

- <u>Levees</u> are <u>raised river banks</u>, made of coarse river load material deposited during <u>floods</u>.

- <u>Estuaries</u> are <u>funnel-shaped river mouths</u>. Most are found where an existing river has had its lower reaches flooded after changes in <u>sea level</u>.

- <u>Deltas</u> form when a river deposits silt <u>too fast</u> for the sea to remove it, and the river splits into lots of <u>distributaries</u>. There are three main types of delta:

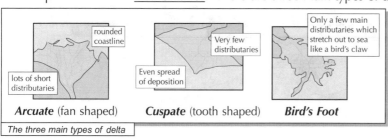

Arcuate (fan shaped) — lots of short distributaries, rounded coastline. **Cuspate** (tooth shaped) — Even spread of deposition, Very few distributaries. **Bird's Foot** — Only a few main distributaries which stretch out to sea like a bird's claw.

The three main types of delta

SUMMARY

River features

Upper stage	Middle and lower stages
Interlocking spurs	Meanders
Waterfalls	Ox-bow lakes
Rapids	Alluvium
V-shaped valley	Flood plain
Potholes	Levees
	Estuaries
	Deltas

EXAMPLES

River	Cause	Type of delta
Nile	Tideless sea (Mediterranean)	Arcuate
Tiber	Large load	Cuspate
Mississippi	Large load	Bird's foot

Glaciation

Ice Ages shaped much of the landscape we know in the UK today.

Many Landscapes were Shaped by Ice

At various stages in Britain's geological history, the climate got colder. These Ice Ages were periods of intense glacial activity. The last started 100 000 years ago, ending 10 000 years ago.

All of Scotland, Ireland, Wales and the north of England were covered by an area of ice. Glaciers (slow-moving masses of ice) were formed which moved down valleys with great erosive power, like giant bulldozers, carving new features.

During that time the southern and eastern parts of the British Isles, which weren't covered by ice, had a climate like the one in modern tundra areas.

Three Ice Actions Changed the Landscape

- Freeze-thaw action (see page 3) is a type of weathering where water settles in cracks in the rock surface, freezes and expands, pressurising surrounding rock. Then it thaws and contracts, releasing the pressure. Repeating the process loosens the surface layer of rock.

- Abrasion is a process of erosion where rock fragments in the ice grind against the rock over which the ice is moving, like a rough sandpaper, wearing away the land.

- Plucking (quarrying) is also a type of erosion. It occurs when meltwater at the base of a glacier freezes on the rock surface. As the glacier moves forward it extracts pieces from the rock surface.

> Glaciers can move solid loads — the load is either frozen in the glacier, carried on its surface, or pushed in front of it, and is deposited when the ice melts at the end of a glacial period.

Glaciers are Similar to Rivers

Rivers and glaciers both start in highland areas — glaciers start when the climate is so cold that winter snow and ice don't melt in summer. Ice builds up in mountain-top hollows — on the colder slopes which don't get much sun.

Both rivers and glaciers flow downhill, although a glacier is slower — 3 to 300 metres per year. A river flows into the sea, while a glacier ends in a snout ('dead ice'), or in the sea.

Both have distinctive cross profiles and long profiles. In both cases, upland areas have erosion features and lowlands have depositional features.

Glaciation

Extent of glaciation over Britain

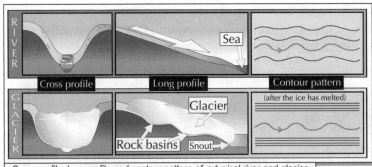

Cross profile, long profile and contour pattern of a typical river and glacier

Glacial Erosion

At certain points in history, Britain has mainly been covered in ice. Glaciers slowly moved over land, carving new features and creating today's landscape.

Glacial Erosion creates Upland Features

Ice in hollows causes <u>plucking</u> and <u>freeze-thaw action</u> which <u>steepen</u> the back and side walls. The ice moves with a circular motion known as <u>rotational slip</u> which deepens the hollow into a bowl shape — a <u>corrie</u>, forming a lip at the valley end.

Once the corrie is <u>full of ice</u> it flows out over the lip and down the valley as a <u>glacier</u>. Where the ice pulls away from the back wall, a Bergschrund (a large crevasse, or crack in the ice) forms.

When the ice <u>melts</u> it leaves these corries — steep-sided, armchair-shaped hollows, often with <u>tarns</u> (lakes) at the bottom.

<u>Two neighbouring corries</u> means glacial erosion narrows and steepens the wall between them, forming a knife-edged ridge or <u>arête</u>.

<u>Several</u> corries and arêtes around a mountain summit form a <u>pyramidal peak</u>.

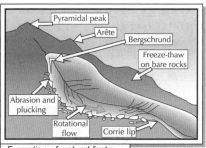
Formation of upland features

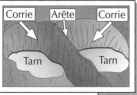
Formation of an arête

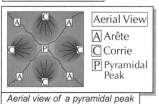

Aerial View
A Arête
C Corrie
P Pyramidal Peak

Aerial view of a pyramidal peak

KEY TERMS

<u>Plucking:</u>
See page 8.

<u>Freeze-thaw action:</u>
See page 3.

The Old Valley is <u>Altered</u> by the Glacier

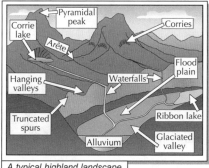
A typical highland landscape

The valley cross-profile changes from a <u>V-shape</u> to a <u>U-shape</u> as the glacier moves down it with great power, eroding slope material. The valley, or glacial trough, becomes a <u>straighter, more linear feature</u>, as the ice doesn't wind round spurs but <u>cuts through</u> them, leaving steep edges on the valley sides — <u>truncated spurs</u>.

<u>Original tributary valleys</u>, which didn't experience such powerful glacial erosion, are now at <u>higher levels</u> than the main valley. Tributary streams enter a valley as <u>waterfalls</u> from <u>hanging valleys</u>. If a tributary glacier joined the main glacier it increased its power to carve a depression. That means that the valley floor often has a <u>river</u> flowing along it, and sometimes a thin <u>ribbon lake</u>, which forms in the <u>rock basin</u> made by the glacier.

<u>Roches moutonnées</u> can also be found on glaciated valley floors. These are small outcrops of resistant rock. Moving ice smooths the up-valley slope by <u>abrasion</u>. A steeper down-valley slope forms by <u>plucking</u> along joints and bedding planes.

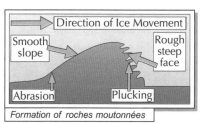
Formation of roches moutonnées

EXAMPLES

Tarn
Red Tarn, Lake District

Arête
Striding Edge, Lake District

Pyramidal peak
Snowdon, Wales

Truncated spurs
Nant Ffrancon, Snowdonia

Ribbon lake
Lake Windermere, Lake District

Glacial Deposits

When the ice melts a variety of deposits are laid down —
either by the glacier itself or by powerful meltwater streams.

Glaciers Produced Moraines, Drumlins and Erratics

Moraines are rock material laid down by
a retreating glacier — there are different
types, depending on their position:
Terminal — the furthest point reached.
Lateral — along the sides.
Medial — at the junction of two glaciers.

Drumlins are elongated hills of glacial
deposits — about 1km long, ½ km wide
and 150 m high. They usually occur in
groups or swarms, called a 'basket of
eggs' topography because of their shape.
They're usually round and blunt on the
upstream end, and tapered and pointed
at the other.

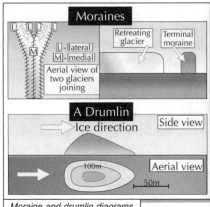

Moraine and drumlin diagrams

Erratics are 'foreign' pieces of rock found in previously glaciated areas —
i.e. they've been moved, often many miles, by a glacier.

Ground moraines (called till or boulder clay) are disorganised piles of boulders,
stones and clays deposited as a glacier melts — they have no distinctive shape.

All glacial deposits are angular and mixed up ('unsorted') — unlike river deposits.

Meltwater Streams left Deposits

Meltwater deposits came from streams in, on and under the ice. These streams
increased in discharge due to the large-scale melting of the ice. They also had
large loads which made new features when they were deposited. All these
features are in sorted, layered deposits.

- Outwash plains are large areas of sand and gravel laid down in
  lowland areas by meltwater streams flowing from an ice sheet,
  sorted into layers consisting of distinctive particle sizes.

- Eskers are long, winding ridges
  of deposited material (many km
  long) laid down in the channels
  of streams in and under the ice.

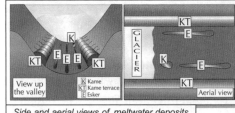

Side and aerial views of meltwater deposits

- Kames are small mounds of
  deposits formed when meltwater
  streams flow over the snout of the
  glacier to flatter ground below.

- Kame terraces are linear features along the sides of valleys where
  meltwater streams deposited their load between the side of the valley
  and the edge of the glacier.

- Kettle holes are found where blocks of
  ice broke off from the glacier as it
  retreated and were buried in the solid
  deposits. When the ice melted, the
  overlying material collapsed to form a
  small depression — a kettle hole.

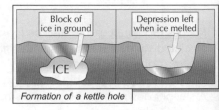

Formation of a kettle hole

Coastal Landforms from Erosion

Wave erosion forms many coastal landforms over long periods of time.

Rock Erosion Forms Cliffs

Waves erode rocks along the shoreline by hydraulic action, corrosion, corrasion (see page 4) and pounding. A notch is slowly formed at the high water mark which may develop into a cave. Rock above the notch becomes unstable with nothing to support it, and it collapses.

The coastline can retreat over many years as this process continues to form a wave cut platform with cliffs behind. The actual size and angle of the cliff will depend on the local rock and its hardness.

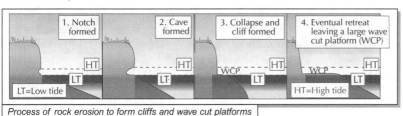
Process of rock erosion to form cliffs and wave cut platforms

Eroded Hard and Soft Rocks form Headlands

If there are alternate bands of hard and softer rock in the coastline, the harder rocks take longer to erode than the softer rocks — because the sea has less effect.

The hard rock will be left jutting out forming one or more headlands — usually with cliffs. The softer rock will be eroded to form bays — the erosion means that the bays will usually slope more gently inland, creating room for a beach to form.

Again, the local geology will affect the actual shape and size of the features formed.

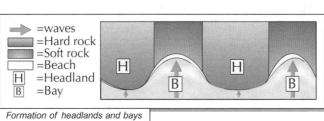
Formation of headlands and bays

Caves, Arches and Stacks can also be Formed

A crack or rock weakness in a headland can be eroded — wave energy is usually strong there because the headland juts out. This forms one or more caves.

Occasionally the pressure of air, compressed in the caves by the waves, weakens the roof along a major joint and the rock collapses to form a blow hole. Further erosion enlarges the cave and it breaks through the headland, forming an arch.

The roof of this arch is often unstable and eventually collapses leaving a stack or series of stacks.

Areas with a limestone or chalk geology are prone to this kind of erosion.

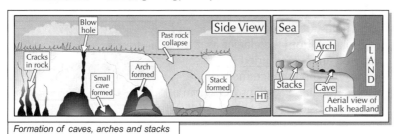
Formation of caves, arches and stacks

EXAMPLES

Wave cut platform

Robin Hood's Bay, Yorkshire

Cliffs

White Cliffs of Dover

Caves

Fingal's Cave, Staffa

Arch

Durdle Door, Dorset

Stacks

The Needles, Isle of Wight

Coastal Landforms from Deposition

Deposition from the sea forms specific coastal landforms.

Beaches are formed by Deposition

Beaches are found on coastlines where eroded material in the sea has been deposited — e.g. in bays between headlands. They vary in size from tiny Cornish inlets to vast stretches like at Blackpool. Beach fragment size depends on local rock type and wave energy.

Storm beaches are ridges of boulders at the landward side of beaches caused by heavy seas piling up material at the high-tide mark.

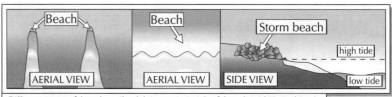

Different types of beach — tiny inlets, vast stretch of beach and storm beach

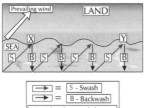
Spits are Long Beaches formed by Longshore Drift

Spits are sand or pebble beaches sticking out to sea, but joined to the land at one end — they are mainly formed by the process of longshore drift, where beach material is transported along the coast by waves breaking at an angle.

Spits tend to be formed across river mouths, where the coast suddenly changes direction, or where tides meet calmer waters of a bay or inlet.

At the spit end there are usually some hooks or recurves formed by occasional strong winds from another direction. Waves can't reach the sea areas behind the spit, so they're often mud flats and salt marshes.

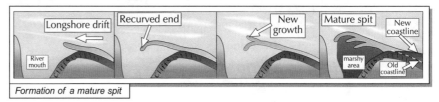

Formation of a mature spit

EXAMPLES

Fine sand beach
Blackpool

Pebble beach
Hastings

Spits
Mouth of River Exe, Devon
Orford Ness, Suffolk

Tombolo
Chesil beach, south coast

Barrier beach
Slapton Sands, S. Devon

Tombolos and Barrier Beaches Join bits of Land together

Tombolos are found where an island is joined to the mainland by a ridge of deposited material, e.g. Chesil Beach on the south coast — this is 18 km long and joins the Isle of Portland to the mainland.

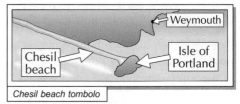

Chesil beach tombolo

Barrier beaches are found where a spit extends right across a shallow bay, e.g. Slapton Sands, South Devon — the water behind it is left as a lagoon which may slowly become a marsh.

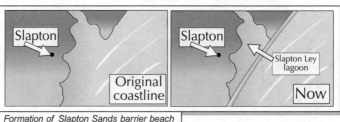

Formation of Slapton Sands barrier beach

Landscapes and People

Certain landscapes are used by <u>people</u> in different ways, often causing conflict. This page focuses on human activity in glacial and coastal landscapes.

Glaciated Highlands Suffer <u>Lots of Conflicts</u>

Glaciated highlands such as the Lake District are used by different people. <u>Farmers</u> grow <u>crops</u> on the fertile valley floors and have <u>sheep</u> on the rocky, unfarmable mountain sides. <u>Tourists</u> enjoy visiting the area for the beautiful <u>scenery</u> and then walking, climbing or sailing. The deep valleys are ideal for building <u>dams</u> for generating <u>hydro-electric power</u> (HEP) and <u>reservoirs</u> for collecting and storing water which can then be <u>piped</u> to drier areas in the south.

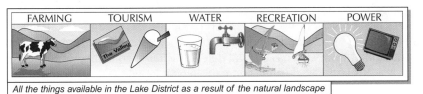

FARMING   TOURISM   WATER   RECREATION   POWER

All the things available in the Lake District as a result of the natural landscape

These different uses cause <u>conflict</u>:

- <u>Water companies</u> conflict with farmers over <u>flooding</u> valley floor farmland, conservationists over <u>ruining</u> the natural countryside, and tourists wanting to use the water for <u>leisure activities</u>.

- <u>Farmers</u> conflict with roadbuilders who <u>use up valuable land</u> for roads and car parks, and tourists who drop <u>litter</u>, leave farm gates open and <u>damage</u> dry stone walls by climbing over them.

- <u>Conservationists</u> conflict with tourists who can damage natural features by footpath erosion, and who need tourist accommodation building.

The National Park Authorities have to <u>balance out</u> the various uses and demands <u>without</u> destroying the resource that is the major attraction in the first place.

<u>Coastal Protection</u> is a Priority

Many coastlines are beautiful so lots of people visit them — but they're <u>fragile</u> and can be damaged by people trampling over them. Some are natural conservation areas with <u>rare habitats</u> which are easily destroyed, e.g. sand dunes.

Coastal areas need to be <u>managed</u> carefully, either by national bodies such as the National Parks Authorities and the National Trust, or by local authorities.

<u>Access</u> is possible with <u>limited disruption</u> and <u>damage</u> — e.g. authorised car parks and picnic sites, well-marked footpaths and information leaflets about erosion. Footpaths can be <u>reinforced</u> and the areas at risk <u>fenced off</u> from the public.

Coastal land use causes many <u>conflicts</u>:

- <u>Residents</u> want to preserve their homes and livelihoods.

- <u>Tourists</u> want access to the coastal areas without restriction.

- <u>Conservationists</u> want to preserve local habitats and protect rare wildlife.

The government has to consider the effect of an action in one place on other places nearby, and also to use public money in the <u>best</u> possible way, benefiting the most people. Coastal protection is very <u>expensive</u> — it's important to spend local authority money in the most economical way, because we can't afford to protect the whole coastline.

EXAMPLES

Glaciated highlands
The Lake District
Snowdonia
Scottish Highlands

EXAMPLES

This reservoir in Snowdonia, Wales is used for hydro-electric power.

TIP

<u>Coasts</u> will probably be affected by <u>global warming</u>:

If global warming carries on as predicted by scientists, <u>ice</u> at the north and south poles will melt, <u>raising</u> the sea-levels all over the world. Coastal defences will have very little effect.

TIP

See <u>page 45</u> for the different ways in which coasts can be protected.

13

Case Studies

For the exam you need to know about the landforms in a particular landscape, and the geomorphic processes that have shaped it — e.g. things like erosion and geology. You also need to think about how humans have affected the landscape. There are three UK example landscapes on this page.

Case Study 1: *River Landscape — River Tees, UK*

The River Tees is found in north-east England. It starts in the <u>Pennines</u> and flows eastwards towards the <u>North Sea</u>. The upper stage has a <u>V-shaped valley</u>, <u>interlocking spurs</u> and a <u>waterfall</u> at High Force. Further downstream, the valley widens and the river starts to <u>meander</u>. Several meanders have been cut through to shorten the journey for boats. At the lowest end of the river, it flows into an <u>estuary</u> where <u>mud flats</u>, such as Seal Sands, have been created by deposition.

The Tees has a history of <u>flooding</u>, which has led to the need for flood defences. The <u>Tees barrage</u> was built to keep the stretch of river between Yarm and Stockton from flooding. Yarm also has a flood defence scheme consisting of <u>reinforced concrete walls</u> with flood gates, and earth <u>embankments</u>.

TIP

See pages 43-45 for more on river and coastal management.

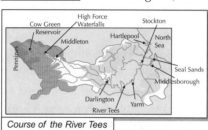

Course of the River Tees

The Tees is also managed to provide a reliable <u>water supply</u>. Cow Green <u>reservoir</u> was built in 1970 to provide water for Teesside's industries. It <u>stores</u> water in times of plenty, which can then be <u>released</u> when the flow is low.

Case Study 2: <u>Coastal Landscape — Holderness, UK</u>

An example of a stretch of coastline with an <u>erosion</u> problem is along the Holderness coast of Yorkshire. This lies between Flamborough Head and Spurn Head. The coastline is made up of soft clay and therefore experiences rapid <u>erosion</u>. In addition, <u>longshore drift</u> moves south along the coastline so there is little opportunity for beaches to become established in front of the cliffs. It has formed the spit at Spurn Head.

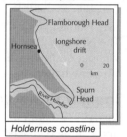

Holderness coastline

Many villages have been eroded away into the sea and <u>lost</u>, but some, such as Mappleton, have recently built expensive <u>coastal defences</u> like sea walls. Some of the coastline is protected in this way, some is allowed to <u>retreat</u> in a <u>controlled</u> way and some is left to <u>nature</u>.

Case Study 3: <u>Glacial Landscape — The Lake District, UK</u>

The Lake District is located in Cumbria in north-west England. It is a <u>mountainous</u> area of beautiful scenery created by glaciation. There are <u>ribbon lakes</u>, such as Lake Windermere, <u>tarns</u> in corries, such as Red Tarn, and <u>arêtes</u>, such as Striding Edge on the mountain of Helvellyn.

The human uses of the landscape are mainly based around <u>tourism</u>, <u>farming</u> and <u>forestry</u>. The Lake District has <u>mountainous</u> parts used by tourists for rambling, walking and climbing. The large <u>lakes</u> also attract tourists who come for boat trips, sailing or water skiing. There are also lots of places to keep tourists busy on <u>rainy days</u>, such as the Aquarium of the Lakes. Tourism needs to be <u>managed</u> properly, or popular places ('honeypot locations') can get <u>overcrowded</u>.

Farming in the Lake District is <u>limited</u> by the landscape but both <u>arable</u> and <u>pastoral</u> farming does take place. <u>Crops</u> are grown on the flat, fertile valley floors. The <u>slopes</u> are used for <u>pastoral</u> farming — mostly sheep farming.

Revision Summary

This section is all about physical geography, so it's more straightforward to learn than some of the other sections. You don't have to worry so much about opinions and debates — you just have to learn some fancy words and diagrams. Have a go at the questions on this page when you feel you know enough.

1) How are extrusive igneous rocks formed? Name an example.

2) Which type of rock are sandstones, clays and shales?

3) Name three examples of metamorphic rocks. How are they different from the original rocks they were formed from?

4) Name the three types of plate margin.

5) At which type of plate margin are fold mountains common?

6) Describe the processes of freeze-thaw and onion-skin weathering.

7) How is limestone weathered? Name the features which might be formed.

8) Write a mini-essay describing how a river changes form from the upper to the lower stage.

9) List and describe the four ways in which rivers erode.

10) Define suspension, saltation, traction and solution.

11) Describe the four main stages of deposition in a river.

12) What are interlocking spurs? How are they formed?

13) Describe the formation of waterfalls and rapids.

14) Describe the formation of meanders and ox-bow lakes.

15) Name and describe three features of the lower stage of a river.

16) Name and describe three ways that ice has changed the landscape.

17) In what ways are glaciers similar to rivers?

18) Describe how three different upland features were formed by glacial erosion.

19) What would a V-shaped valley look like after a glacier had passed through?

20) Describe the following features: a) truncated spurs   b) hanging valleys
    c) ribbon lakes   d) roches moutonnées.

21) What might be found in a 'basket of eggs' topography?

22) Name and describe three types of meltwater deposit.

23) Explain how a wave cut platform with cliffs behind would be formed.

24) Draw a rough diagram to show the formation of caves, arches and stacks.

25) Name the process which leads to the formation of spits.

26) What is the difference between a tombolo and a barrier beach?

27) Write a mini-essay to discuss the different uses of a glaciated highland, explaining how they might lead to conflict.

28) Describe the conflicts that might occur over the issue of coastal protection.

29) Describe the human influences on the River Tees.

30) What are the main causes of erosion on the Holderness coastline? What is being done to improve the situation?

31) Describe the human uses of the Lake District.

EXAM TIP

There are loads of diagrams in this section — the best way to learn them is always just to copy them out again and again. You might think you know them because they look familiar when you're reading a page, but that doesn't mean you'll be able to recreate them in the exam.

Local Weather and Microclimates

A <u>microclimate</u> is where there are <u>local differences</u> in <u>climatic features</u>. This page explains the difference between urban and rural microclimates and the factors which influence microclimates.

Urban and Rural Areas have <u>Different Microclimates</u>

- Urban areas have a <u>higher average</u> temperature than the surrounding countryside — up to 4 °C at night and 1.6 °C in the day. This is called the '<u>Urban Heat Island Effect</u>'. It happens because buildings act like <u>storage heaters</u> absorbing the Sun's heat during the day and letting it out at night. Also, the air is full of <u>pollutants</u>, which acts as a blanket at night to stop heat getting out. In addition, heat is <u>added</u> to the air from things like central heating, factories and power stations.

- <u>Sunshine levels are lower</u> in urban areas due to tall buildings and fog. There's more <u>cloud</u>, <u>rain</u> and <u>fog</u> as the high level of pollutant particles in the air act as <u>condensation nuclei</u> (this basically means water forms around them).

- <u>Humidity is lower</u> in urban areas as the warmer air can hold more moisture.

- Wind speed is generally <u>reduced</u> by tall buildings in urban areas. However, a <u>wind tunnel effect</u> can occur, for example if the buildings are in rows. This <u>increases</u> wind speed.

<u>Other Factors</u> Affect Local Microclimates

<u>Colour of surface</u>: Dark surfaces absorb <u>more heat</u> than light ones. Light surfaces <u>reflect more heat</u> from the sun.

<u>Aspect</u>: If a place <u>faces</u> the Sun it will receive <u>more heat</u> than one in <u>shadow</u>. In the <u>northern hemisphere</u> slopes which face the <u>south</u> are warmer than those which face north.

<u>Proximity to water</u>: Areas near water like lakesides and coasts are <u>more humid</u>, with more cloud and rain. Water creates little friction to stop air movement so places near water tend to be windy. Because water temperature changes more slowly than land temperature, areas near water have a smaller temperature range.

Factors which affect microclimate

<u>Surface cover</u>: Bare surfaces are <u>windier</u>, because they have little friction to interrupt air flow. They have larger daily and annual <u>ranges of temperature</u> than vegetation-covered surfaces. They are also <u>drier</u> because there is less interception and evapotranspiration.

<u>Vegetation</u>: Areas with a lot of vegetation are humid because of evapotranspiration. They tend to be sheltered places because the leaves and branches act as wind-breaks. The floor of a forest is usually cool because the leaves block out sunlight.

<u>Exposure</u>: Exposed areas like hilltops are cooler than sheltered ones because wind has a cooling effect.

<u>Altitude</u>: Temperatures fall by about 1 °C for every 100 m above sea level so higher areas are cooler. Higher areas are also wetter because of <u>relief rainfall</u>.

Regional Weather Patterns in the UK

This page explains the spatial and seasonal variations of the climate in the UK.

The _Climate_ of the British Isles is _Seasonal_

In the UK we have cool, wet winters and warm, wet summers. The correct term to describe this is a cool temperate maritime climate. The climate in the UK isn't always the same — it varies spatially (in different places) and temporally (at different times). The map below shows the causes of the main trends of the climate in the UK.

SEASON
In summer it's warmer than in winter because during summer, the Sun is at a higher angle in the sky. In the winter, the Sun moves south in the sky so the amount of daylight hours the UK has in winter is lower than in the summer.

PRECIPITATION
Snow is most common on the highest ground in the UK. The north and west of the UK have higher snowfall than the south and east, especially the mountainous areas. The UK doesn't have a distinguishable rainy season but there is slightly more rainfall in the winter and the north has more rainfall than the south.

> **FACT**
>
> The variation in climate across Britain has lots of consequences e.g. —
> - Different crops are grown in different places because of climate.
> - Different types of tourism are located in different places e.g. resorts on the south coast attract people who want to be in the sun whilst other people go skiing in Scotland.

RELIEF
Altitude affects regional climate. The high mountainous areas have lower average temperatures than the lowland areas. Mountains in the west like the Lake District and Snowdonia are also wetter, because they bring relief rainfall as saturated air moves in from the Atlantic Ocean (see page 18).

> **TIP**
>
> Practise drawing a rough outline of the British Isles without copying from an atlas. If you can draw the basic shape then you'll be able to make use of it in the exam — it's often quicker to draw and annotate a map than write a few paragraphs.

Scottish Highlands

Lake District

Snowdonia Peak District

North Atlantic Drift

Areas of the UK

LATITUDE
The southern parts of the UK are warmer than the northern parts because of their lower latitude. The further you move towards the equator the warmer it is. This is because the Sun is at a higher angle in the sky near the equator, so the sunlight has to travel through less atmosphere to reach the Earth.

> **TIP**
>
> Remember that latitude means how far north or south of the equator a place is. Longitude is how far east or west of Greenwich a place is.

LONGITUDE
The west of the UK is warmer than the east. This is because there is a warm ocean current called the North Atlantic Drift, which flows towards the west of the UK from the Gulf of Mexico.

Precipitation in the UK

The UK gets a lot of <u>precipitation</u>. Precipitation is any moisture that falls from clouds — rain, snow, hail and drizzle.

Three Types of *Rainfall* are Common in the *UK*

Precipitation happens when water in the atmosphere cools. At <u>dew-point</u> the air is <u>saturated</u> and water vapour <u>condenses</u> to form tiny droplets of water which make up <u>cloud</u>. The droplets get bigger, until they fall as <u>precipitation</u>.

All the rainfall in the UK is one of three types:

Relief Rainfall Happens When Clouds Meet *Mountains*

<u>Relief rainfall</u> — If warm, wet, onshore winds reach a <u>mountain barrier</u> they have to <u>rise</u> over it. The air <u>cools</u> and the water vapour <u>condenses</u>. Clouds are formed and precipitation starts. When the air reaches the <u>summit</u> the drier air <u>descends</u>.

The air becomes <u>warmer</u> as it descends and any remaining clouds <u>evaporate</u>. This drier area is known as a <u>rain shadow</u>. Yorkshire is in a rain shadow.

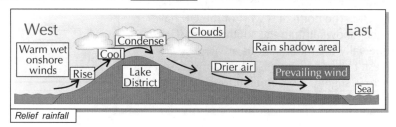

Relief rainfall

Convectional Rainfall is Where the *Sun Heats* the *Earth*

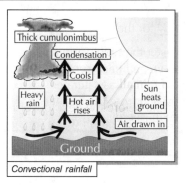

Convectional rainfall

<u>Convectional rainfall</u> — The Sun <u>heats</u> the ground and warm air <u>rises</u> vertically. As it rises it <u>cools</u> until <u>condensation point</u> is reached. This leads to thick cumulonimbus clouds being built up by strong thermal up-currents, which produce <u>low pressure</u> (see page 19).

This low pressure causes air to move into its centre — rainfall is heavy and intense and is sometimes accompanied by <u>thunder</u> and <u>lightning</u> due to the electrically unstable conditions.

Frontal Rainfall is Where *Warm* and *Cold* Air *Meet*

<u>Frontal rainfall</u> — A <u>low</u> is formed where <u>warm</u> and <u>cold air</u> meet. This causes <u>condensation</u> and <u>frontal rain</u>, which can be in the form of <u>light drizzle</u> or <u>heavy rain</u> depending on its <u>position</u> in the low.

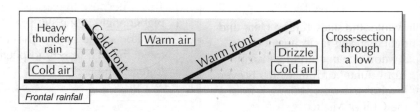

Frontal rainfall

Highs and Lows and the UK Climate

High and low air pressure cause different types of weather.
The UK gets a mixture of highs and lows.

Lows *Cause 75% of UK Weather*

Lows (or <u>depressions</u>) form to the west of the UK. Warm, wet <u>tropical maritime</u> air from the south meets <u>cold polar</u> air from the north along the <u>Polar Front</u>.

The warmer, less dense air is forced to <u>rise above</u> the colder air resulting in 'less' air at the Earth's <u>surface</u>. An area of <u>low pressure</u> occurs. This low with its <u>warm</u> and <u>cold fronts</u> moves north-east across the UK bringing an associated pattern of weather conditions with it.

> **EXAM TIP**
>
> **Remember, weather fronts are only associated with lows — not with highs.**

Lows Bring a <u>Definite</u> Series of <u>Weather Conditions</u>

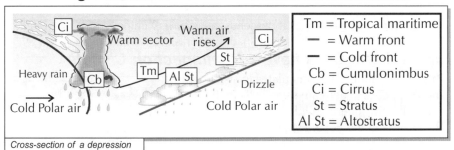

Tm	= Tropical maritime
—	= Warm front
—	= Cold front
Cb	= Cumulonimbus
Ci	= Cirrus
St	= Stratus
Al St	= Altostratus

Cross-section of a depression

As a low approaches, it starts to <u>drizzle</u>.
It rains more <u>heavily</u> as the <u>warm front</u> approaches.

When the warm front passes, the rain stops, the weather becomes <u>brighter</u>, and the <u>clouds disappear</u>. The <u>temperature rises</u>, due to being in the <u>warm sector</u>.

About 12 hours on, it gets <u>windier</u> and <u>colder</u>. Clouds build up as the <u>cold front</u> moves in. <u>Heavy rain</u> falls and it's <u>cold and windy</u> for the next few hours.

The cold air behind the cold front often moves <u>faster</u> than the warm air, and often <u>overtakes</u> and <u>undercuts</u> the warm sector, giving an <u>occluded front</u> — no warm sector but a longer period of continuous rainfall.

After the rain, conditions may <u>settle</u> for a short while before the <u>next</u> low or high. As the cold front passes the wind changes direction (veers) from warm southerly to cool north-westerly.

SUMMARY

Effects of lows and highs

Lows (depressions)	Highs (anticyclones)
Unstable conditions	Stable conditions
Rain	Clear skies
Wind	Heat waves in summer
Low temperatures	Cold night temperature
Possible occluded	in winter
fronts	Fogs

Highs are Linked to <u>Clear Skies</u>

Highs (or <u>anticyclones</u>) usually bring <u>clear</u> skies and <u>stable</u> conditions, lasting for days or weeks.

In summer they're associated with dry, hot (25 °C) weather — our '<u>heat waves</u>'.

In winter the skies can be <u>clear</u> and <u>bright</u>, causing rapid <u>heat loss</u> by radiation at night, and <u>low</u> night temperatures with heavy frosts even though the days are sunny.

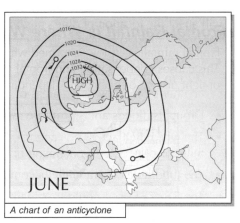

JUNE

A chart of an anticyclone

FACT

Anticyclones can cause <u>temperature inversions</u>, where the temperature near the ground is colder than above. This can produce persistent fogs known as <u>anticyclonic gloom</u>.

World Climate Zones

Each part of the Earth's surface is classified as belonging to a specific climatic zone, according to the weather conditions most commonly associated with it.

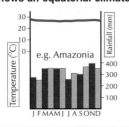
The World has Several Climatic Zones

Classification is based on maximum and minimum temperatures and the temperature range, as well as total and seasonal distribution of precipitation.

Because we can see climatic patterns, there must be influencing factors at work — atmospheric cells are an example.

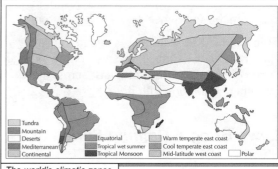

Tundra
Mountain
Deserts
Mediterranean
Continental
Equatorial
Tropical wet summer
Tropical Monsoon
Warm temperate east coast
Cool temperate east coast
Mid-latitude west coast
Polar

The world's climatic zones

Atmospheric Cells have a Big Impact on Climate

The world's atmosphere circulates in six systems known as cells. There are three cells in the northern hemisphere and three in the southern. They're called the Polar, Hadley and Ferrel cells.

The equator receives more of the Sun's energy than the poles — the cells are the Earth's way of moving excess energy from the equator to the poles. In the cell systems warm air rises and travels towards a pole before it cools and descends. This has two influences on climate:

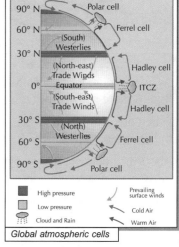

90° N — Polar cell
60° N — Ferrel cell
(South) Westerlies
30° N
(North-east) Trade Winds — Hadley cell
0° Equator — ITCZ
(South-east) Trade Winds — Hadley cell
30° S
(North) Westerlies
60° S — Ferrel cell
90° S — Polar cell

High pressure
Low pressure
Cloud and Rain
Prevailing surface winds
Cold Air
Warm Air

Global atmospheric cells

- They cause prevailing winds (winds that blow most commonly in a particular area).
- Weather systems form where the cells meet.

The Inter Tropical Convergence Zone (ITCZ) is the zone where the trade winds meet — the air is heated and it rises to form the Hadley cells. Huge clouds are formed which cause thunder storms at high altitude and gentle doldrum winds at ground level. The ITCZ shifts throughout the year as the position of the midday Sun in the sky moves between the Tropic of Cancer and the Tropic of Capricorn.

Global Climate is Changing

There is evidence to suggest that our global climate is slowly changing, which will affect the location of different climate zones. Some of this climate change has been linked to human activity increasing global warming (see page 33).

- Ice-sheets and glaciers are beginning to melt. Sea levels have risen by 0.25 m in the last 100 years. In the next 100 years, they will probably rise another 0.5m. Low-lying areas of the world are under threat of flooding.
- Droughts, floods and storms are more severe, widespread and common.
- The wheat belt across N. America, Europe and Asia, which provides grain for millions of people, is becoming drier and less productive.
- The tundra belt is gradually becoming warmer.
- The Sahara Desert could eventually spread north into southern Europe.
- The North Atlantic Drift could be altered, and the UK could get much colder.

Case Studies

For the exam you need to know about the UK climate (which is all on pages 17 - 19). You also need to know about two climates which are different from the UK so this page has case studies on Nigeria and Japan.

Case Study 1: <u>Nigeria — A Tropical Continental Climate</u>

Nigeria's climate is <u>tropical continental</u> (TC) . Nigeria does have a coastline but the influence of the African landmass is much greater than the effect of the Atlantic Ocean. The centre of Nigeria is about <u>10° north</u> of the equator. Nigeria has two distinct seasons — a <u>hot dry season</u> and an even hotter <u>wet season</u>.

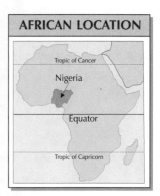

AFRICAN LOCATION

Tropic of Cancer

Nigeria

Equator

Tropic of Capricorn

<u>Winter is the hot dry season</u>

- In the winter months, the tilt of the Earth and its orbit of the Sun mean that there is slightly less daylight time and the Sun's angle is reduced in the sky.

- During the winter months, it is dry and hot. This is because the <u>prevailing winds</u> are the warm <u>North East Trade Winds</u> which blow from the Sahara.

- These winds have descended from the <u>Hadley Cell</u> and have already given up their moisture so they bring dry conditions.

<u>Summer is the hotter wet season</u>

- In the summer months, the Sun is more directly overhead and brings with it a change in <u>prevailing winds</u>.

- The <u>Inter Tropical Convergence Zone</u> (ITCZ), which is a band of low pressure, is over Nigeria in the Northern Summer.

- The Sun forces air to rise, causing <u>convection currents</u> which bring precipitation — this is Nigeria's <u>wet season</u>.

TIP

If you get a question about contrasting climates, the easiest thing to do is compare either Nigeria or Japan with the UK. It's always best to write about ones you've revised.

The movement of the ITCZ is <u>not the same</u> every year and sometimes it <u>fails</u> to move to Nigeria at all. When it fails Nigeria misses its rainy season and there are <u>droughts</u>. The changes in the movement of the ITCZ may be the result of climate change caused by human activity (see page 20).

Case Study 2: <u>Japan — A Warm Temperate Climate</u>

Japan has quite a complicated climate. It is a long country which means that its latitude varies considerably over its length. There are large seasonal and spatial variations in climate across Japan:

- In general, the climate is <u>warm temperate</u>, especially in the southern islands of <u>Kyushu</u> and <u>Shikoku</u>. The south has <u>long hot summers</u> and <u>mild winters</u>. Southern Japan is warmer than southern Britain because it's closer to the <u>tropics</u>. There is also more precipitation.

- Although Japan's climate is <u>influenced by the continental mass of Asia</u>, the warming influence of the <u>Pacific Ocean</u> is responsible for the key features of the Japanese climate.

- <u>Heavy rains</u> fall in July and September. They are caused by the <u>low pressure</u> over the <u>Asian land mass</u>. As air rises over the continent moist air from the Pacific Ocean rushes north, bringing rainfall.

- <u>Typhoons</u> (see page 31), which are typified by <u>strong winds</u> and <u>torrential rainfall</u> happen in <u>September</u> and they increase Japan's precipitation totals.

- Japan has a different precipitation pattern to the UK because the majority of its precipitation falls within the <u>typhoon season</u>. In the British Isles the precipitation is distributed more evenly throughout the year.

JAPANESE LOCATION

Hokkaido

Honshu

Shikoku

Kyushu

Revision Summary

Climate isn't as easy as you might think — there are lots of complicated things to learn and it's easy to get mixed up. These questions are designed to make you think about the hard things that all seem a bit the same. Basically, if you repeat these questions until you can do them all then you'll stand a good chance of doing well if you get a question on the atmosphere or climate in the exam.

1) Define the term 'microclimate'.

2) What is the urban heat island effect?

3) Why does Los Angeles have bad air quality?

4) Is humidity highest in urban or rural areas?

5) What effects can tall buildings have on wind speed in urban areas?

6) Name seven factors which can affect microclimates.

7) How much does temperature tend to decrease for every 100 m above sea level?

8) Where is snow most common in the British Isles?

9) Write a short paragraph to describe the UK climate.

10) How does latitude influence climate?

11) What ocean current influences the British climate?

12) Name the three types of rainfall that are common in the British Isles and give a place where each one is found.

13) What is 'dew-point'?

14) What percentage of British weather is caused by lows?

15) Describe the different types of weather that occur as a low passes.

16) What type of weather is associated with a summer high?

17) What type of weather is associated with a winter high?

18) What is a 'temperature inversion'?

19) What factors are used to classify climates?

20) Name the three types of atmospheric cell.

21) What is 'continentality'?

22) What is a prevailing wind?

23) What might some of the consequences of global climate change be?

24) Draw a location map for Nigeria.

25) Write a mini-essay to describe what the climate is like in Nigeria.

26) What are the two southern islands of Japan called?

27) When is the Japanese typhoon season?

28) How does the pattern of precipitation in Japan differ from Britain's?

EXAM TIP

Atmospheric cells are probably the most difficult thing in this section so don't worry if you don't get them straight away. A good way to learn them is to practise copying out the diagram on page 20 and adding the labels on. Even if you can't get it perfectly, just correctly using phrases like ITCZ and the names of the cells will get you marks in the exam.

The Hydrological Cycle

The <u>hydrological cycle</u> is the movement of a constant amount of water between the <u>sea</u>, <u>land</u> and <u>atmosphere</u>. It's a continuous cycle with no start or end point.

<u>Evaporated</u> Sea Water Forms the <u>Inputs</u> to the System

<u>Winds</u> containing evaporated sea water blow towards land where they rise, leading to <u>cloud</u> formation and <u>precipitation</u> like rain, snow or hail to fall on the ground below.

Then the Water <u>Flows</u> Through the System via <u>Transfers</u>

There are two kinds of transfer you need to know about — <u>vertical</u> and <u>horizontal</u>.

<u>Vertical transfers:</u>
Water <u>collects</u> on plant leaves — this is called <u>interception</u>. Then it drips off and enters the soil. It can then <u>filter through</u> the soil through spaces in the surface layers — this is called <u>infiltration</u>. The water can also move <u>downwards</u> through the ground at deeper levels, until it reaches the water table — this is called <u>percolation</u>.

<u>Horizontal transfers:</u>
There are <u>four</u> kinds of <u>horizontal transfer</u> that you need to know about:

- <u>Surface run-off</u> is when water flows overground to rivers, lakes or the sea.

- <u>Channel flow</u> is the flow of water in a stream, river or lake.

- <u>Through flow</u> is when <u>infiltrated water</u> moves through <u>soil</u> to a river.

- <u>Groundwater flow</u> is when <u>percolated water</u> moves below the water table to a river.

The water cycle

Some Water is <u>Stored</u> in the System

There are <u>four</u> kinds of <u>storage</u> that you need to know about:

- <u>Channel storage</u> happens in <u>rivers</u> and <u>lakes</u> and is vital for our <u>water supply</u>.

- <u>Groundwater storage</u> occurs in <u>underground rocks</u> which are porous. This means they <u>collect water</u> in the pores, which are spaces between their particles.

- <u>Soil water storage</u> is when water is stored in the <u>soil</u> and is used by <u>plants</u>.

- <u>Short-term storage</u> occurs after interception on things like <u>plant leaves</u> and in puddles.

Evaporated Water is the <u>Output</u>

There are three ways that water can get back into the atmosphere:
- <u>Evaporation</u> happens when sea, lake or river water is heated by the <u>sun</u>. The water vapour <u>rises</u>, then <u>cools</u> and <u>condenses</u> to form <u>clouds</u>.
- <u>Transpiration</u> is when <u>plants</u> lose moisture.
- <u>Evapotranspiration</u> is both evaporation and transpiration together.

Drainage Basins

All river systems have their own drainage basin.

A *Drainage Basin* is a Land Area Drained by a River

Catchment area and drainage basin mean the same thing — the land area from which a river and its tributaries collect the rainwater passing from the soil and rock. The land provides the water source for the main river and all its tributaries.

The size of the catchment area depends on the size of the river. A watershed is high ground separating two neighbouring drainage basins. On one side of the watershed the water drains in one direction, and on the other side it drains the opposite way.

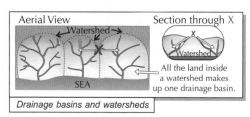

Drainage basins and watersheds

A Drainage Basin Works as a *System*

Water enters the drainage basin as precipitation. It goes through a series of flows and stores before reaching the sea as river run-off. The time between rain and river run-off depends on the characteristics of the basin — e.g. its shape, size, rock type and vegetation.

Energy is put into the system by the steepness of the hills / valley and the force of gravity. Water moves rock and soil material through the drainage basin system. It's picked up when the water energy is high and deposited when energy is low.

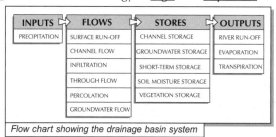

INPUTS ▷	FLOWS ▷	STORES ▷	OUTPUTS
PRECIPITATION	SURFACE RUN-OFF	CHANNEL STORAGE	RIVER RUN-OFF
	CHANNEL FLOW	GROUNDWATER STORAGE	EVAPORATION
	INFILTRATION	SHORT-TERM STORAGE	TRANSPIRATION
	THROUGH FLOW	SOIL MOISTURE STORAGE	
	PERCOLATION	VEGETATION STORAGE	
	GROUNDWATER FLOW		

Flow chart showing the drainage basin system

A River Basin has Several Important *Features*

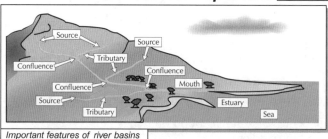

Important features of river basins

- The source is where a river starts, usually in an upland area.

- A tributary is a stream or smaller river that joins the main river.

- A confluence is the point where two rivers join.

- The mouth is where the river flows into the sea.

- An estuary is where the mouth is low enough to let sea enter at high tide. This causes deposition, forming mud banks, which the river flows between.

FACT

Drainage basins can be vast. For example, the Amazon drainage basin covers much of Brazil. In combination the Ganges and Brahmaputra rivers drain an area six times the size of Britain.

EXAM TIP

See page 14 for the River Tees case study.

EXAM TIP

Using the correct terms to describe drainage basins will save time in the exam and impress the examiners.

Flooding and Storm Hydrographs

Storm hydrographs are used to study the flow of rivers
and predict when floods are likely.

You Need to Know how to <u>Use</u> the Storm <u>Hydrograph</u>

The graph shows the <u>change in river discharge</u> (volume of water
flowing per second) over a <u>short period</u> of time after a storm.
It's used to work out when a flood might be coming.

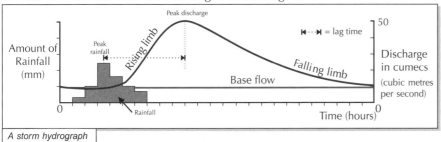

A storm hydrograph

TIP

Remember, river discharge
is always measured in
<u>cumecs</u>, which are cubic
metres per second.

- The <u>base flow</u> is the <u>normal discharge</u> of the river.
- The <u>rising limb</u> represents the <u>increase in discharge</u> after the storm.
- The <u>falling</u> or <u>recession limb</u> represents the <u>decrease in discharge</u>.
- The <u>lag time</u> is the <u>amount of time</u> between <u>peak rainfall</u> and <u>peak discharge</u>.

The river is likely to <u>flood</u> when the graph is <u>steep</u>. This is because there is a
rapid increase in discharge over a short period of time — the river system is
unable to transport it away before it floods onto the surrounding land.

FACT

There is always a delay
between peak rainfall and
peak flow because it takes
a while for all the water
that falls in the drainage
basin to get into the river
channel.

Several Factors Affect the <u>Steepness</u> of the Graph

The <u>steeper</u> the graph, the <u>more likely</u> the river is to flood:

FACTOR	STEEPER ⌒		GENTLER ⌒	
1. Total Rainfall	High		Low	
2. Intensity of Rain	High	(runs off)	Low	(soaks in)
3. Wetness of Ground	Saturated	(runs off)	Dry	(soaks in)
4. Rock Type	Impermeable	(runs off)	Porous	(soaks in)
5. Ground Cover	Bare Soil	(runs off)	Vegetated	(soaks in)
6. Slope Angle	Steep	(runs quickly)	Gentle	(runs slowly)

Factors which affect the shape of the hydrograph

FACT

Increased vegetation
leads to a gentler graph
because some of the
water is intercepted which
prevents it getting into
the river channel.

Floods can Cause <u>Extensive Damage</u>

The amount of damage caused by a flood depends on where it happens, how
severe it is and how well prepared people are to deal with it. Floods can cause
extensive damage and disruption because they affect many different things:

TIP

See page 37 for more
about the damaging
effects of flooding.

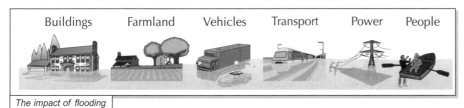

Buildings   Farmland   Vehicles   Transport   Power   People

The impact of flooding

Ecosystems

<u>Ecosystems</u> are all the living and non-living things sharing a certain <u>environment</u>, and how they work together as a system.

An *Ecosystem* is a System of *Linked Parts*

The linked parts of an ecosystem (e.g. animals, plants and their habitats) interact in the ecosystem in a series of <u>inputs</u>, <u>outputs</u>, <u>stores</u>, <u>flows</u>, <u>processes</u> and <u>cycles</u> For example, a <u>tropical rainforest</u> (TRF) ecosystem has these links:

- The main input is heat and light from the <u>Sun</u>.
  The Sun also triggers a cycle of activity that leads to <u>rainfall</u>.

- The weather (Sun and rain) sustains the dense <u>vegetation</u> of the rainforest.

- The rainforest's continuing leaf fall builds up a carpet of <u>debris</u> which decays to provide <u>nutrients</u> for fresh growth.

- <u>Animals</u> and <u>insects</u> help with the scattering of seeds, the pollination of plants and the decay of leaf litter.

- Rainforest plants are <u>eaten</u> by insects, birds and animals, which are in turn eaten by larger animals. Native rainforest <u>people</u> eat both the plants and the animals, in <u>harmony</u> with the ecosystem, not taking more than they need.

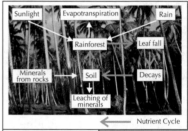

The TRF ecosystem

A *Food Chain* is a Series of *Links* in an *Ecosystem*

Most food chains start with <u>green plants</u> which are called <u>primary producers</u> as they use the Sun's energy to <u>photosynthesise</u>, i.e. make their food.

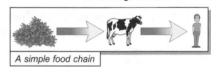

A simple food chain

Plants also take up <u>minerals</u> (from rock breakdown) from the <u>soil</u>. Some animals known as <u>herbivores</u> eat these plants. Other animals known as <u>carnivores</u> eat the herbivores and other carnivores.

<u>Organisms die</u> and nutrients return to the soil when bacteria and fungi <u>decompose</u> (break down) the dead material making it ready for <u>re-use</u>. This means the process goes in a <u>cycle</u>.

There are *Two Main Natural Cycles* in an *Ecosystem*

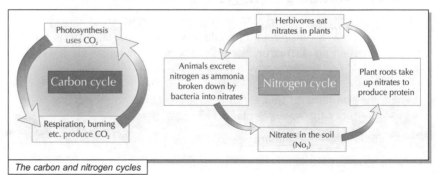

The carbon and nitrogen cycles

Changing Ecosystems: TRFs

Ecosystems can change both by natural processes and human activity. The large-scale removal of trees (deforestation) is one example of how humans can change ecosystems. It is a problem in many TRFs, like the Amazon rainforest in Brazil.

Trees in <u>Brazil</u> are Disappearing for <u>Five</u> Reasons

<u>Logging</u> for export to MEDCs — trees should be <u>replanted</u> so the industry can keep selling <u>long-term</u>, but many LEDCs want to make money today and don't plant for the future.

<u>Population</u> is <u>increasing</u> — <u>settlement</u> and <u>road-building</u> in the TRF are needed.

The forest is cleared to set up <u>cattle ranches</u> which quickly make land useless.

<u>Mineral extraction</u> helps Brazil pay <u>foreign debts</u> — Carajas in Brazil is the world's largest iron reserve.

<u>Hydro-electric power</u> has led to large areas of land being <u>flooded</u>.

There are Two Sides to the <u>Deforestation Debate</u>:

For Conservation	For Deforestation
• <u>Agricultural development</u> is pointless — soils robbed of TRF lose fertility, so farming can't continue after three or four years.	• <u>Poverty</u> means a country needs to use all resources to help its people.
• <u>Medicinal products</u> have been found in TRFs before — they could be destroyed before they're discovered.	• Many <u>MEDCs</u> destroyed their <u>own forests</u> when developing — the UK did (although not so fast) — so they shouldn't have one rule for themselves and one for LEDCs who need to develop.
• <u>Heritage value</u> means preserving this ecosystem for future generations — there are many native tribes whose way of life is being destroyed.	• Nearly 75% of world carbon dioxide emissions comes from <u>MEDCs</u> — why should LEDCs have to change policy first?
• Removing the forest means more <u>global warming</u>.	• MEDCs should <u>lower interest</u> or <u>cancel debts</u> if they're so worried about deforestation.
• Forest removal lowers <u>evapotranspiration</u> and rainfall — altering the climate.	• MEDCs are <u>buying</u> the products of these areas — so why should LEDCs stop?

<u>Deforestation</u> Affects the TRF Ecosystem

The TRF is a very <u>fragile</u> environment, and deforestation starts a chain of events affecting the <u>processes</u> and <u>stability</u> of the ecosystem:

- The felling of trees cuts off the <u>nutrient</u> supply to the now exposed soil.
- The heavy daily rainfall easily <u>washes away</u> the now loose, crumbly soil.
- The <u>rivers</u> get blocked with red silty material, which causes <u>flooding</u>.
- Where the soil remains intact, nutrients are washed down into the earth (<u>leached</u>), out of the reach of plants or crops.
- The soil becomes <u>infertile</u> and supports little growth.
- <u>Evaporation</u> and <u>evapotranspiration</u> are reduced by deforestation, so <u>rainfall</u> in the area is reduced, also making plant growth less likely.

Case Study

The Amazon Basin of Brazil is an example of a tropical rainforest ecosystem. Learn this case study of the links between climate, vegetation, soils and people.

Case Study: *The Amazon Basin Ecosystem, Brazil*

Climate:

The climate is dominated by <u>high temperatures</u> all year round. The average temperature is about 26 °C, a figure which only varies by 2 or 3 degrees over the year. This means there is a <u>continuous</u> growing season.

<u>Rainfall</u> is high at more than 2000 mm a year. It generally falls <u>all year</u> round, although further from the equator, towards the edge of the forest, there is a short dry season. The high <u>humidity</u> in the forest area means that it rains heavily every day, usually in the afternoon.

Vegetation:

The vegetation is dominated by <u>deciduous</u> trees, constantly growing and shedding leaves at different times. There are no obvious <u>seasons</u>, so flowers, fruits and seeds are available all year round.

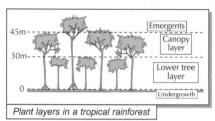

Plant layers in a tropical rainforest

The trees form three distinctive <u>layers</u>. The emergent tallest trees are over 45 metres in height. The <u>canopy layer</u> lies below at about 30 metres. Below that is a thinner, <u>lower</u> tree layer. There is only sparse <u>undergrowth</u> as little light gets through the tree layers.

The trees grow <u>shallow roots</u> and a broad spread of <u>buttress roots</u> develops above the ground. These give added stability. Leaves are thick and <u>waxy</u>, cutting down on moisture loss through transpiration. They also have <u>drip-tips</u> to help the heavy daily rainfall run off quickly.

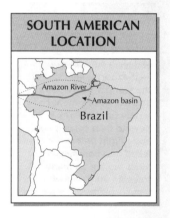
Soils:

Brazil's TRF

Soils are mainly red and rather clay-like. They are rich in iron and aluminium oxides which are left after the heavy rain has <u>leached</u> out other materials and nutrients. The soil itself is largely <u>infertile</u> when the nutrients stored in the living things are removed. The poor, loose structure is easily washed away when exposed to the heavy rains.

A thick carpet of fallen, decaying <u>leaves</u> builds up on the forest floor. It rapidly <u>decomposes</u> due to warm, humid conditions and decomposing bacteria, and makes a <u>fertile</u> top layer of soil. So despite the poor soil underneath, there are plenty of nutrients available in the top layer for the dense vegetation.

People:

Some native people are <u>hunter-gatherers</u>, while a larger number live by a form of <u>shifting cultivation</u> which involves cutting small farming areas into the forest. Shifting cultivation, or 'slash and burn', is <u>wasteful</u> as the plots are only of any value for a few years before the soil loses <u>fertility</u> and is <u>eroded</u>. The farmers move on to repeat the process nearby.

There is pressure from logging, mining, ranching, electrical power schemes and commercial crop production in the forest, so <u>deforestation</u> is happening. This is a problem for both the <u>environment</u> and the <u>native people</u> who are being forced out of their homes.

Revision Summary

This section isn't over until you've been through some questions to see how much you know. When you've finished, do them again, and keep trying them until you can do them all without needing to peek at the book.

1) Name the input to the hydrological cycle.

2) What are interception, infiltration and percolation?

3) List the four types of horizontal transfer in the hydrological cycle.

4) Explain the difference between groundwater and soil water storage.

5) How can water get back into the atmosphere?

6) What is a drainage basin?

7) Sketch a diagram to show how drainage basins and watersheds interact.

8) What does the time taken between rain and river run-off depend on?

9) List three flows and three stores in the drainage basin system.

10) Draw a rough diagram of a river, marking on it the terms source, tributary, confluence, mouth and estuary.

11) What does a storm hydrograph show? What is it used for?

12) Why is there always a delay between peak rainfall and peak flow?

13) What would the storm hydrograph look like if the river was likely to flood?

14) List six factors which affect the steepness of the storm hydrograph.

15) Name four different things that floods affect.

16) Define the term 'ecosystem'.

17) What role does the Sun play in a TRF's ecosystem?

18) How do plants and animals interact in the TRF's ecosystem?

19) What are primary producers? Why are they important to an ecosystem?

20) Explain what happens in the carbon and nitrogen cycles.

21) What is deforestation?

22) List five reasons why deforestation happens.

23) Write a mini-essay to discuss the pros and cons of deforestation.

24) What is Malaysia's policy on deforestation?

25) Give five effects of deforestation on the ecosystem of the TRF.

26) Describe the climate of the Amazon rainforest in Brazil.

27) Name the three tree layers in a TRF.

28) How does the TRF's poor soil support such dense vegetation?

29) What is 'shifting cultivation'? Is it good for the land?

30) What are the causes of deforestation in the Amazon rainforest?

EXAM TIP

You'll never find out how much you really know unless you test yourself with practice questions. It's a good idea to ask your teacher for extra questions to try as part of your revision.

Short-Term Weather Hazards — Fog

Fog is made up of water droplets suspended in the air.
The droplets often form around dust or smoke particles.

There are <u>Five Main Types</u> of Fog

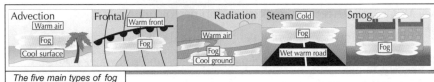

The five main types of fog

- <u>Advection fog</u> is caused when warm, moist air blows (is advected) over a cooler surface, <u>reducing</u> lower air layer temperature. It's common in <u>summer</u> over cool seas.

- <u>Frontal fog</u> is due to the <u>fine drizzle</u> which occurs along a <u>warm front</u> — rain falls through the cold sector from the warm air above. The cold air is <u>saturated</u> causing condensation and fog.

- <u>Radiation fog</u> occurs in a <u>shallow layer</u> on <u>low-lying ground</u> at night or early morning. The ground <u>cools</u> by radiation overnight. The layer of air above the ground is chilled to <u>dew-point</u>, condensing the moisture into fog. It's common in areas with moist air, a clear night sky (maximum heat loss) and a slight breeze to spread cooling upwards — usually <u>temperate latitudes</u> in spring, autumn and winter.

- <u>Steam fog</u> forms where <u>cold air</u> is over <u>warm water</u>. The warm vapour <u>condenses</u> producing a wispy steam, e.g. on a cold morning over a lake. Very cold air produces <u>ice fog</u> containing <u>ice crystals</u>.

- <u>Smog</u> occurs mostly in urban areas. It is produced when air contains lots of <u>smoke</u> and <u>pollution</u>, giving many 'condensation nuclei'. <u>Condensation</u> occurs around these even if the air is <u>unsaturated</u> — making smog <u>dense</u> and <u>long-lasting</u>.

Fog Affects <u>Human Activities</u>

Fog is a local atmospheric hazard — it makes travelling <u>dangerous</u>:

- Thick fog can cause <u>road accidents</u> and <u>motorway pile-ups</u>. Motorway drivers can now be warned of fog by special lit-up <u>signs</u>. <u>Lights</u> have also been fitted on sections of motorway known to be prone to fog. These additions have helped <u>reduce</u> the number of fog-related accidents.

- Fog also affects <u>air travel</u>. Planes are fitted with automatic landing devices, so they can still <u>land</u> in fog. However, sometimes the fog affects <u>visibility</u> so much that the pilots can't move planes to and from the terminal. This leads to flights being <u>cancelled</u> or <u>diverted</u> to other airports.

- In heavy fog, <u>ships</u> risk crashing into rocky <u>outcrops</u> that they would normally be able to see. <u>Lighthouses</u> prevent them crashing into these outcrops at night, but in the fog, the light is less <u>visible</u> — so lighthouses have <u>foghorns</u> that ships can hear instead.

Lighthouses are less visible in fog

Hurricanes are another short-term atmospheric hazard. They're areas of intense low pressure which only occur in certain parts of the world.

Hurricanes Form Over Warm, _Tropical_ Seas

Hurricanes start within 8° and 15° north and south of the Equator. They form over seas when the temperature is higher than 26°C.

They usually occur in late summer and early autumn. They tend to move westwards once formed and polewards when they reach land.

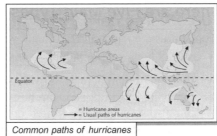

Common paths of hurricanes

The exact cause of hurricanes is uncertain. As they form over warm, moist sea, their energy probably comes from water evaporating rapidly at a high temperature.

The rising air cools and water vapour condenses releasing huge amounts of heat — this heat then provides enough power to drive the storm. Hurricanes rely on plenty of warm, moist air from the sea — they die out over land.

Hurricanes Bring _Extreme Weather_ and _Damage_

A hurricane's life-span is about 7 to 14 days — but it's only in one place for a few hours. It's an intense upward spiral or vortex of warm air.

An affected area experiences three main stages of the storm. During the first (A), there will be strong winds and rain.

The central part (B) is called the eye. It's 30 to 50 km across and is produced by descending air — the weather there is calm, with light winds and no rain.

After the eye has passed, conditions in the final stage (C) are similar to stage A.

Cross-section through a hurricane

The winds and rain are strongest in the area immediately surrounding the eye.

Hurricanes cause considerable damage:

- High winds can cause damage to buildings, crops, power supplies, etc.

- Ocean storm surges can flood areas, especially in densely populated areas.

- Heavy rainfall can cause flooding and other damage to homes and crops.

Effects are often more serious in LEDCs than in MEDCs due to limited resources, for example, emergency services and storm-proof housing.

FACT

Tornadoes are similar to hurricanes but form over level land areas, e.g. the US plains. A tornado is a violent, whirling vortex of air with a funnel-shaped cloud above. It can cause large-scale damage along a path 150 metres wide and 10 km long.

Advance Warning of Hurricanes is Now Possible

Modern technology like satellite photography can track hurricanes to tell us when and where they'll strike next. These kind of warnings help people to take precautions.

During a storm, it's important to stay inside. Even if you go out during the eye of the storm, you could get caught out when the winds and rains start up again. Afterwards, roads, water, gas and electricity should not be used until the all-clear is given.

EXAMPLE

The USA uses warnings with different levels, based on the likelihood of a hurricane and when it could strike — e.g. one level gives a 50% chance of a hurricane in the next 36 hours, another says one is due in the next 12 hours.

Medium-Term Hazards — Forest Fires

Forest fires are a medium-term 'terrestrial hazard' (i.e. caused on the Earth's surface rather than the atmosphere) — they last longer than hurricanes but, unlike global warming, they are not long-term hazards (see page 33).

Forest Fires have Two Main Causes

Forest fires are caused in two main ways:

- Naturally through a lightning strike.

- Through human activity, e.g. careless use of camp fires or dropped cigarettes. Forest fires can also sometimes be started deliberately.

The fire's progress is increased when there is dry leaf litter or dead wood and a strong wind.

Forest fire in action

FACT

The summer of 2003 was extremely hot in Europe, with higher than average temperatures recorded in many countries.
This contributed to serious forest fires that devastated areas of countries such as Portugal, Italy, France and Spain.

Forest Fires happen in Warm, Dry Places

Forest fires usually occur in areas with a warm, dry climate. Areas with a Mediterranean climate such as Colorado and California in the USA and Portugal in Europe are particularly prone to fires.

Fires can occur in other areas of the world if the conditions are right, e.g. the UK during summer drought conditions.

Forest Fires have Devastating Effects

Forest fires kill plants, animals and even people. Soil is damaged and plants and animals are killed.

Fires can last for days, weeks or even months depending on the environmental conditions and the action of firefighters. Sometimes rainfall is the only way a fire will be extinguished.

The effects of forest fires are sometimes positive. New plants thrive in the spaces created in the forest, with no competition for light from taller trees, and nutrients are put back into the soil by the ash. Regular fires help to reduce the collection of dead wood and lessen the likelihood of a larger forest fire.

WORLD LOCATION

Australia

Australia Suffered from Drought and Fires in 1994

Australia is a very dry country — two-thirds of it is desert-like, receiving very little rain. It often has droughts and bush fires, so the natural vegetation has adapted to these harsh conditions. Some species of Australian plant even need fire to release their seeds. Despite the dry climate, the scale of Australia's drought and bush fires in 1994 was unexpected.

AUSTRALIAN LOCATION

In January 1994, following lower rainfall levels than usual, there were hundreds of uncontrollable fires raging around Sydney. 1.25 million acres of bush were destroyed, including 90% of the Royal National Park. The fires destroyed homes, schools, roads, rail and telephone lines. Thousands of people had to be evacuated from Sydney's suburbs. Many species of native Australian animals were also affected — hundreds of wallabies, emus, koalas and possums were killed.

Australian bush

The <u>average global temperature</u> has <u>risen</u> by over ½ °C in the last hundred years — and the years since 1980 have been the hottest on record.

The Earth is like a <u>Giant Greenhouse</u>

<u>Energy</u> from the <u>Sun</u> passes through the <u>atmosphere</u> as light and <u>warms</u> up the <u>Earth</u>. When the energy is radiated and <u>reflected</u> back off the surface as <u>heat</u>, it's <u>trapped</u> by the atmosphere and <u>can't get back out</u> into space — like how a <u>greenhouse</u> keeps the heat inside. Increasing greenhouse gases in the atmosphere (e.g. carbon dioxide and methane) increases the problem, so the Earth gets <u>hotter</u>.

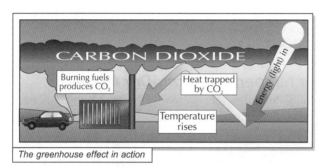

The greenhouse effect in action

Human Activity Increases Global Warming

- Since the <u>Industrial Revolution</u>, people have needed more <u>energy</u> for work and in the home — this has come from burning more <u>fossil fuels</u>, particularly coal and oil. This <u>burning</u> releases more <u>carbon dioxide</u> and <u>methane</u> into the atmosphere.

- Global warming is reduced by trees using up carbon dioxide in photosynthesis — so <u>deforestation</u> increases global warming.

- Decomposing <u>rubbish</u>, <u>cattle grazing</u> and <u>rice growing</u> all increase the output of methane into the atmosphere.

There's <u>Conflict</u> Over Reducing <u>Greenhouse Gases</u>

Global warming has been linked to climate change and potentially serious consequences for humans, e.g. a rise in sea level (see page 20 for more on the effects of climate change). To prevent further global warming, greenhouse gas emissions need to be <u>reduced</u>, but some countries disagree over whether to, for different reasons:

- Many countries use fossil fuels but want to <u>reduce</u> gas emissions.

- <u>India</u> and other <u>LEDCs</u> don't want to reduce emissions, because their <u>rate of development</u> would <u>slow down</u>.

- <u>Oil states</u>, such as those in the Gulf, don't want to reduce emissions because their <u>revenues</u> from <u>oil sales</u> would <u>decrease</u>.

- <u>The USA</u> is reluctant to reduce emissions because it doesn't want a fall in <u>living standards</u>. For example not using fossil fuels would affect transport and industrial processes, both of which use a large amount of fossil fuels.

Tectonic Hazards

Tectonic hazards such as earthquakes and volcanoes
are caused by the movements of tectonic plates.

EXAM TIP

This page shouldn't be
read alone. Don't forget to
read page 2 to find out
about the different types
of plate margin.

Tectonic Plates are Bits of the Earth's Crust

The Earth's <u>crust</u> lies on top of a mass of molten rock called <u>magma</u>.
This magma produces hot rising and falling currents called <u>convection
currents</u>. The Earth's crust is split into separate <u>tectonic plates</u>, which
are <u>moved</u> in different directions by the convection currents.

Where plates meet, at <u>plate margins</u>, the movement causes <u>tectonic
hazards</u> like earthquakes and volcanoes, and also the formation of
fold mountains and deep ocean trenches.

Volcanoes and *Earthquakes* Occur *Near* Plate Margins

The two maps below show the main <u>plate boundaries</u> and where <u>volcanoes</u>,
<u>earthquakes</u> and <u>fold mountains</u> are found. Look how they match up —
they must be connected because the patterns are so similar.

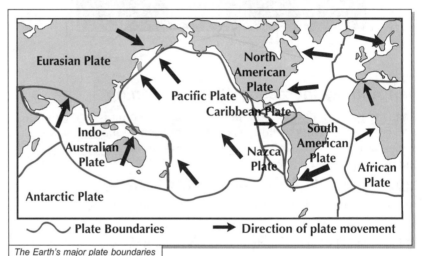

The Earth's major plate boundaries

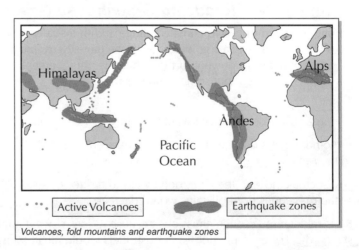

Volcanoes, fold mountains and earthquake zones

FACT

There are over 600 active
volcanoes in the world
today — the greatest
concentration is around
the Pacific Ocean in the
'Ring of Fire'.

Tectonic Hazards — Earthquakes

Tectonic plates floating slowly around sounds fairly safe. But when the plates come together you can get <u>earthquakes</u> — which aren't so great.

Earthquakes Occur at *Compressional* or *Transform* Plate Margins

As two plates move towards each other, one can be pushed down under the other one and into the mantle. If this plate gets stuck it causes a lot of <u>strain</u> in the surrounding rocks. Sideways-moving plates can also get stuck.

When this tension in the rocks is finally released it produces strong shock waves known as <u>seismic waves</u>. This is an earthquake.

The shock waves spread out from the <u>focus</u> — the point where the earthquake starts. Near the focus the waves are stronger and cause more damage.

The <u>epicentre</u> is the point on the Earth's surface immediately above the focus.

EXAMPLES

Recent major earthquakes			
Place	Year	Deaths	Size on Richter Scale
Seattle	2001	0	7.2
India	2001	20,000	7.7
Turkey	1999	10,000	6.7
Kobe (Japan)	1995	5,000	7.2

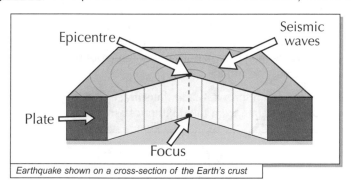

Earthquake shown on a cross-section of the Earth's crust

(Epicentre, Seismic waves, Plate, Focus)

The *Richter Scale* Measures Earthquakes

The size or <u>magnitude</u> of an earthquake is measured using a <u>seismometer</u>, a machine with a <u>seismograph</u> on a revolving drum. Earthquake vibrations are recorded by a sensitive arm with a pen at the end which moves up and down.

These readings are measured using the <u>Richter scale</u> for energy released, which is an open-ended scale.

The Richter scale is a <u>logarithmic scale</u> — which means that an earthquake with a score of 5 is ten times more powerful than one with a score of 4. One with a score of 4 is ten times more powerful than one that scores 3, and so on.

The most serious earthquakes are in the range of 5 to 9. The Richter scale goes on forever but no earthquakes above 9 have ever been recorded.

EXAMPLE

The earthquake in San Francisco in 1906 was the most powerful in the last couple of centuries, reading 8.6 on the Richter scale.

EXAM TIP

The damage caused by an earthquake isn't just about the Richter scale reading. It also depends on how strong the buildings are and how well prepared people are to deal with it.

Noted on seismometer | Faint tremor felt | Buildings damaged | Some buildings collapse | Distinct shaking | Large buildings destroyed | Can see ground shake

0 1 2 3 4 5 6 7 8 9 10

LOG SCALE

The Richter scale, showing examples of impact

Tectonic Hazards — Volcanoes

Volcanoes are often (but not always) <u>cone shaped</u>, formed by material from the <u>mantle</u> being forced through an opening in the Earth's crust, the <u>vent</u>.

EXAMPLES

Extinct Volcano
Devil's Tower, Wyoming, USA

Dormant Volcano
Santorini, Greece

Active Volcanoes

Place	Last Eruption
Mount Etna, Sicily	2001
Montserrat, West Indies	1997
Pinatubo, Philippines	1991
Mount St. Helens, USA	1980

Volcanoes are <u>Extinct</u>, <u>Dormant</u> or <u>Active</u>

Volcanoes are split into three different categories depending on how likely they are to erupt.

<u>Extinct</u> volcanoes are those which will never erupt again.

<u>Dormant</u> volcanoes are those which haven't erupted for at least 2000 years. (Of course, just because a volcano is described as dormant, that doesn't mean it will never erupt again.)

<u>Active</u> volcanoes have erupted recently and are likely to erupt again.

A <u>Composite Volcano</u> is made up of <u>Lava</u> and <u>Ash</u>

Four different types of substance can be ejected through the vent — <u>ash</u>, <u>gas</u>, pieces of rock known as <u>volcanic bombs</u>, and <u>molten rock</u>. Molten rock is known as <u>magma</u> when it's under the ground, and <u>lava</u> when it reaches the surface.

Once this material has been thrown out at the surface, it <u>cools</u> and <u>hardens</u>, forming the volcano mountain from the mixture of ash and lava.

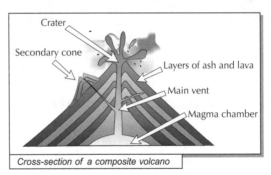

Cross-section of a composite volcano

EXAMPLES

Composite Volcano
Mount Etna, Sicily

Shield Volcano
Mauna Loa, Hawaiian Islands

Dome Volcano
Mount St. Helens, USA

<u>Shield</u> and <u>Dome</u> Volcanoes are made of <u>Lava Only</u>

Volcanoes made up from just hardened lava are known as one of two types, named for the shape of hill they produce:

<u>Shield</u> volcanoes: where the lava is <u>basic</u> (alkaline) and runny. It flows quickly and easily, spreading over large areas to form <u>wide</u>, <u>flat features</u>.

<u>Dome</u> volcanoes: where the lava is acid and thicker. It flows more slowly and hardens quickly to form <u>steep-sided features</u>.

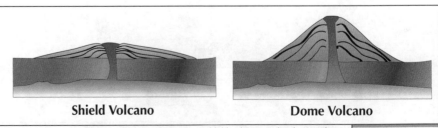

Cross-sections showing the difference between a shield volcano and a dome volcano

Flooding Hazards in MEDCs and LEDCs

Floods can never be good news, but the effects are generally <u>worse</u> in <u>LEDCs</u>. However, there can be serious consequences in MEDCs too.

An MEDC _Flood Example_ — Lynmouth, Devon 1952

There was <u>no early warning system</u> in spite of known <u>high peak discharges</u> (see page 25), so the signs of an imminent flood went unnoticed.

Rapid run-off (so short lag time)

1.75cm rainfall per hour

Saturated

High water table

The causes of the Lynmouth flood

The resulting flood caused <u>casualties</u> and <u>damage</u>:

34 dead   1000 homeless   90 buildings destroyed   150 cars/boats lost

The results of the Lynmouth flood

<u>Other events</u> caused by the flood include:

- <u>Blocked bridges</u> made <u>temporary dams</u> which later <u>burst</u> causing a <u>twelve-metre-high wave</u> to move downstream at 30 km/h causing a lot of damage.

- <u>Boulders</u> weighing up to seven tonnes were <u>carried down</u> the flooded river.

- Near the mouth, the river had been <u>channelled</u> into a <u>culvert</u> in the town, making a <u>narrow outlet</u> to the sea. This man-made channel <u>couldn't cope</u> with the <u>extra discharge</u> so the river <u>changed direction</u> and made its own exit to the sea — causing more damage.

In an _LEDC_ like _Bangladesh_ Floods are _Even Worse_

Some <u>LEDCs</u> use river flooding to cover farmland with <u>fertile alluvium</u> and to provide water for <u>irrigation channels</u> — e.g. the Ganges Valley and Bangladesh delta. However, flood disasters can cause serious damage in LEDCs because their flood <u>preparation</u>, <u>defence</u> and <u>recovery</u> are all lacking, compared to MEDCs.

- <u>Severe floods</u> can destroy food supplies, homes, etc. <u>Emergency services</u> and <u>money</u> are <u>limited</u> in LEDCs, which slows recovery.

- In <u>1988</u>, Bangladesh experienced its worst floods in memory. 7 million homes were destroyed and over 2000 people were <u>killed</u>.

- Floods are often completely <u>unexpected</u>. They usually happen in <u>flatter</u>, <u>lower-lying</u> valleys which are <u>built up</u> and <u>heavily populated</u>.

Human Activity Increases the Risk of Flooding

Human activity can increase the risk of <u>flooding</u> by increasing the rate of <u>surface run-off</u>. This means that water gets into rivers <u>faster</u>, increasing the risk of flooding. There are four main ways in which this happens:

<u>Deforestation</u> means there's no <u>interception</u> of rain by trees.
<u>Cities</u> are designed to <u>channel away</u> water causing increased run-off.
<u>Over-grazing</u> can lead to bare, hard earth with increased run-off.
<u>Draining wetlands</u> means there's nowhere for water to be <u>stored</u> before it reaches the river.

UK LOCATION

Lynmouth

EXAM TIP

Remember — examiners like real examples because they show you understand how theories work in the real world.

WORLD LOCATION

Bangladesh

ASIAN LOCATION

India

Bangladesh

Bay of Bengal

Drought

Water shortage leads to two massive hazards which affect millions of people across the world — <u>drought</u> and <u>desertification</u>.

Drought — When <u>Rainfall</u> Doesn't Meet People's Needs

Drought doesn't just mean low rainfall — in some parts of the world there is <u>always</u> low rainfall and the people <u>adjust</u> accordingly.

Drought occurs when <u>much less</u> rain falls than would <u>normally be expected</u>.

Drought Affects <u>MEDCs</u> and <u>LEDCs</u> Differently

Drought can be devastating to agriculture, as lack of water for <u>irrigation</u> causes <u>crop failure</u>. This leads to loss of income and, in LEDCs that rely on subsistence farming, it causes malnutrition and starvation. In extreme cases, <u>famine</u> occurs — starvation on a massive scale.

In some LEDCs, like <u>Belize</u> in Central America, water shortages are worsened by hotels catering for <u>tourists</u> from MEDCs. They use lots of water to meet the demands of their guests.

In MEDCs low rainfall means that water supplies drop. <u>Reservoirs</u> are rarely full, <u>river flows</u> are down and <u>ground water</u> levels fall steadily. Whilst the amount of water <u>available</u> in the UK has decreased in the last few decades, <u>demand</u> from industry and the public has increased.

MEDCs can cope well with drought because they have better water <u>storage facilities</u> and people don't rely on <u>subsistence crops</u>. Drought is far worse in LEDCs. Often the only way for people to survive is to accept <u>foreign aid</u>.

Drought leads to <u>Desertification</u>

Desertification is where grasslands and forest are turned into <u>desert</u>.   The <u>Sahel</u> region in Africa has turned from savanna to desert and scrub. <u>Long-term drough</u> is the main cause of <u>desertification</u> but the effects are made worse by <u>people</u>.

<u>Soil erosion</u> is gradually turning the land to desert. (See page 46 for more.)

| Overgrazing leaves the ground bare. | The bare soil gets eroded and dried out. |

Overcultivation of the land removes all the nutrients from the soil, leaving it bare.

The grassland turns into desert.

DESERT

Desertification of the savanna grassland

There are <u>three</u> ways in which people contribute to desertification:

* <u>Increased population</u> means more <u>water</u> is used up, <u>more trees</u> are cut down for fuel, and <u>larger herds</u> overgraze the land — vegetation is removed and the ground is left bare, causing <u>soil erosion</u>.

* <u>Climate fluctuations</u> — several years of adequate rainfall encourages farmers to <u>enlarge herds</u> and <u>grow crops</u>. If dry years follow, the land <u>can't support</u> the increased herds and <u>soil erosion</u> occurs.

* <u>Commercial agriculture</u> uses <u>valuable water</u> and pushes subsistence farmers onto marginal land that cannot support farming.

Methods like planting <u>hedges</u> and farming in a <u>less intensive</u> way can help to prevent desertification in areas which are at risk.

Recently scientists have discovered that desertification isn't always permanent. If the land is carefully <u>managed</u> it can slowly <u>recover</u> and vegetation can <u>regrow</u>

EXAMPLE

**Effects of drought in
Ethiopia, 1983-84:**

* **500 000 people died,
mostly of starvation**
* **many people migrated
from remote areas to
refugee camps in Sudan**
* **Ethiopia is still reliant
on aid from foreign
governments and
charities**

EXAM TIP

It's worth mentioning in
your exam answer that
solving the major
problems of civil wars
and overpopulation
would help prevent
desertification a huge
amount — but these are
very hard to deal with.

Environmental Problems and LEDCs

Many LEDCs have significant <u>environmental problems</u> that slow down the development process — lots of LEDCs are in tropical regions and often face hazards because of their climate.

Natural Hazards Cause LEDC Development Problems

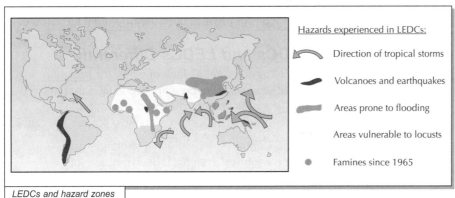

Hazards experienced in LEDCs:

→ Direction of tropical storms

Volcanoes and earthquakes

Areas prone to flooding

Areas vulnerable to locusts

● Famines since 1965

LEDCs and hazard zones

EXAMPLES

In Asia, monsoon winds bring heavy rain, which regularly causes flooding.

Tropical storms (or hurricanes) are common in Asia and the Caribbean.

Large continental land masses have <u>extreme climates</u> and interior areas are very hot with long dry seasons. <u>Water supply</u> is a problem and <u>soil erosion</u> is a constant threat to farming.

<u>Tropical storms</u> (or hurricanes) <u>destroy</u> crops and buildings — repair costs can be enormous.

<u>Rainfall is uneven</u> during the year. Near the equator, communication links can be <u>washed away</u> in the rainy season — tropical countries have wet and dry seasons <u>instead</u> of summer and winter.

Volcano erupting

All <u>natural hazards</u> like <u>earthquakes</u>, <u>volcanoes</u>, <u>tsunamis</u>, <u>droughts</u> and <u>floods</u> cause major damage in many LEDCs. <u>Poor warning</u> and <u>prediction systems</u> lead to many <u>deaths</u> and lots of <u>damage</u> to property. Farmland and development schemes can be destroyed or set back.

LEDCs are Vulnerable to <u>Two Other Factors</u>:

<u>Tropical diseases</u> like malaria spread quickly in LEDCs — the malarial <u>mosquito</u> is responsible for more human deaths than any other creature. <u>Water-borne diseases</u> like bilharzia are also common. Poor diet leads to <u>malnutrition</u> and diseases such as kwashiorkor (a condition affecting children) and rickets. <u>Bad sanitation</u> and <u>polluted water</u> can lead to typhoid and cholera. Recently, <u>AIDS</u> has been an increasing concern.

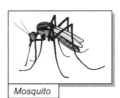

Mosquito

FACT

The rise of AIDS in LEDCs is a massive concern.
Many educational projects have been set up to try and prevent the spread of the HIV virus, which causes AIDS.
Simply informing people about how the HIV virus is transmitted (e.g. through sex) and advising them about preventative measures (like using condoms) can help a great deal.

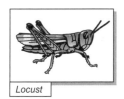

Locust

Pests are a problem in LEDCs, where farmers <u>can't afford</u> pesticides. One of the worst pests is the <u>locust</u> — a grasshopper-like creature that travels in swarms which can eat up entire harvests within hours.

Revision Summary

This section has been all about natural hazards — fog, hurricanes, forest fires, global warming, earthquakes, volcanoes, flooding and drought. When you're happy with what you know, have a go at these questions.

1) Give the definition of fog.

2) Name the five different types of fog and describe how they are caused.

3) What have been introduced to make road, air and sea travel safer in fog?

4) What is the most likely cause of hurricanes?

5) Describe, in order, what you would experience if a hurricane passed over.

6) Is advance warning of hurricanes possible?

7) List the two most likely causes of forest fires.

8) In which type of climate are forest fires most likely?

9) Describe the effects of the bush fires in Australia in 1994.

10) How does the Greenhouse Effect happen?

11) Why don't LEDCs, oil states and the USA want to reduce gas emissions?

12) What are tectonic plates and how do they move?

13) Draw a sketch map of the world's plate margins.

14) What is the 'Ring of Fire'?

15) Name the point where an earthquake starts, and the place above it on the surface.

16) If an earthquake had a Richter scale score of 5, how many times more powerful is it than one with a score of 4?

17) Name two examples of past earthquakes, and give their Richter scale scores.

18) What is a composite volcano made from?

19) Describe the similarities and differences of shield and dome volcanoes.

20) Name two examples of past volcanic eruptions.

21) Write a mini-essay describing the effects of the flood in Lynmouth in 1952.

22) Why are the effects of flooding often worse in LEDCs than in MEDCs?

23) Describe the effects of the flood in Bangladesh in 1988.

24) How do deforestation and over-grazing increase the likelihood of flooding?

25) Give the definition of drought.

26) Why can MEDCs cope with drought better than LEDCs?

27) Explain the three ways in which people contribute to desertification.

28) Draw a sketch map showing the distribution of the world's natural hazards.

29) Name two diseases common to LEDCs.

30) Name the pest which is a particular problem for farmers in LEDCs.

EXAM TIP

Don't just learn what the natural hazards are, make sure you can also say how people are involved:

- How are people affected?
- How do people make the hazard worse?
- What can people do to make the hazard less of a problem?

Surviving Tectonic Hazards

As well as knowing how earthquakes and volcanic eruptions ('tectonic hazards') occur, you also have to know how the hazards affect people, and how people try to cope with the dangers.

People Live in _Earthquake_ and _Volcanic Zones_

You may find it hard to believe, but millions of people live in places which could be devastated by tectonic hazards. Some people have no choice about where they live, and others just don't want to move. Even if everyone who lives in a tectonic zone wanted to leave, there would be problems because more desirable areas are already over-crowded.

Some people live where there are tectonic hazards because they are confident that modern technology will enable scientists to predict hazards. They hope that they will have enough time to leave before an earthquake or eruption.

As well as the risks of living in tectonic areas there are quite a few benefits. For example, volcanic ash creates very fertile soils and geothermal energy can be used to heat homes, water and greenhouses. Tourists are often interested to see the effects of volcanoes and earthquakes so hazards can be important sources of income for some regions.

Scientists Try to _Predict Hazards_ in Advance

It's possible to monitor the tell-tale signs that precede a volcanic eruption. Things such as tiny earthquakes, rising magma, escaping gas, increased magma temperature and changes in the tilt of volcano sides all mean an eruption is likely.

Earthquakes are harder to predict but there are some clues like changes in well water levels, gas emissions, new cracks in rocks, and strange animal behaviour.

Computers are used to analyse past data to forecast future eruptions and earthquakes.

EXAMPLE

Scientists monitoring Mt St Helens, an active volcano:

Good Planning Reduces the Effects of a Hazard

- Monitoring helps predict when hazards are coming so people can be warned.

- Emergency supplies of water and power can be organised in advance. Families can organise supplies of food, dust masks, spare clothes, basic medical supplies, shelters, torches, batteries, mobile phones and other useful items.

- Local emergency services such as the police, fire brigade and ambulance service can be well prepared to deal with any hazard.

- Information on emergency procedures can be made available to the public — e.g. in school classes, meetings for adults, leaflets, newspaper adverts etc. Simply sheltering under a table or avoiding standing next to walls can save someone's life.

- Buildings and roads can be designed to cope with earth movements, so they don't collapse under the strain. For example, new skyscrapers in earthquake zones can be built with a computer controlled counterweight, cross-bracings and special foundations to reduce the impact of an earthquake.

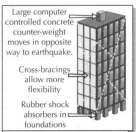

Large computer controlled concrete counter-weight moves in opposite way to earthquake.

Cross-bracings allow more flexibility

Rubber shock absorbers in foundations

An earthquake-proof building

EXAMPLE

Strengthening roads and railways doesn't always help reduce damage. For example, in the 1995 Kobe earthquake the Bullet Train track bent unexpectedly.

Effects of Tectonic Hazards

Earthquakes and volcanoes are a nightmare anywhere,
but they cause <u>more problems for LEDCs</u>.

Three Factors affect How Serious the Disaster is:

- <u>Rural / urban areas</u>: Rural areas have fewer people and
  buildings so the scale of the disaster is smaller.

- <u>Population density</u>: The more people there are, the more deaths.

- <u>How prepared countries are</u>: How ready a country is depends on
  how developed it is. LEDCs have less time, money and expertise
  to prepare for hazards. MEDCs are better prepared but they still
  can't stop disasters happening. They can just limit the damage.

MEDCs can put Emergency Plans Into Action

- Local authority <u>experts</u> assess the seriousness of the situation and the damage

- Local <u>citizens</u> are kept <u>informed</u> — they need to be told what to do next.

- <u>Immediate emergencies</u> have to be dealt with <u>first</u>.
  All casualties are taken to hospital and fires are put out.

- <u>Disrupted public services</u> such as power, water supply and sewage disposal
  have to be <u>restored</u> as soon as possible because there is a risk of <u>disease</u>.

- <u>Communications</u> such as roads, bridges, railways and telephones
  may have been damaged, and <u>mending</u> these is top priority so that
  <u>help</u> from outside the area can get in.

- The efforts of <u>individuals</u>, <u>governments</u> and <u>NGOs</u> (Non-Governmental
  Organisations) such as <u>Oxfam</u> and <u>Cafod</u> have to be coordinated.

LEDCs are Not so Well Prepared...

It is very difficult to warn people about hazards in LEDCs because
communications are poor. The <u>governments</u> have many problems to deal
with so they often don't have the time or resources to make <u>emergency plans</u>.
This means, when a hazard occurs, LEDCs usually suffer major damages and
take a while to get back to normal:

- There are <u>few experts</u> available to <u>assess</u> the situation.

- <u>Without plans</u> there will be <u>delays</u> dealing with the fires, injured people, etc.

- <u>Homes</u> are often built of <u>less sturdy</u> material, meaning
  <u>more damage</u> is likely and <u>fires</u> can spread quickly.

- <u>Limited communications</u> mean people still don't know what's happening.
  There will also only be a few ambulances and fire engines available.

- <u>Water</u> and <u>power supplies</u> are normally <u>poor</u> and mending them is difficult.

- <u>Roads and transport systems</u> are poor to start with, so it's <u>difficult</u> to bring in
  supplies of food, medicine, clothes, shelter etc., even if these are available.

- <u>Lack of money</u> means they have to rely on
  <u>foreign aid</u> which takes <u>time</u> to reach them.

- <u>Medical facilities</u> are <u>limited</u> so many people die of <u>injuries</u> or
  <u>diseases</u> linked to dirty water supply and poor living conditions.

Flood Control — Hard Engineering

Rivers can cause great damage when they flood. There are various strategies for minimising the damage. Hard engineering involves building structures like dams to control the river system.

Dams can Control Discharge for a Whole Valley

Dams and reservoirs in the upper parts of a drainage basin are very effective for controlling the discharge lower down the valley — where the flood threat is greatest. Dams are expensive to build so recently multi-purpose schemes have been built, including hydro-electric power (HEP) stations and recreational lakes — e.g. at Kielder in Northumberland.

All the river sediment is deposited in the reservoir instead of on the floodplain downstream. This means the floodplain is less fertile, forcing the farmers to use more fertiliser. Also, coastal beaches and deltas (see page 7) lose their sediment.

The sediment-free water released by the dam increases erosion downstream. This increases the width of the river, causing problems for bridges and buildings near the river.

The River's Shape can be Changed to Control Flooding

Increasing the capacity of the channel means it can hold more water in a flood.

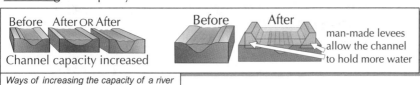

Channel capacity increased   man-made levees allow the channel to hold more water

Ways of increasing the capacity of a river

Culverts straighten and line the river channel to increase the speed of the river and remove excess water more quickly down the channel to the sea.

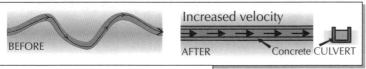

Increased velocity   Concrete CULVERT

Culverts mean water flows to the sea more quickly

Building branching channels off the main river removes the excess water in three ways:

- Taking water to a neighbouring basin with a cut-through.

- Diverting extra water into storage areas on the flood plain.

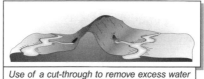

Use of a cut-through to remove excess water

- Building relief channels round towns to hold the excess water.

Hard Engineering can Cause Problems

- Beautiful countryside can be spoiled by ugly buildings.

- Good farmland can be destroyed if upper valley floors are flooded.

- Channels need regular dredging to stop the channel size decreasing.

- Increased channel speed causes flooding and erosion downstream.

- The engineering often looks ugly and affects the natural river ecosystems.

- If a dam, levee or cut-through breaks there could be a big, sudden disaster.

EXAMPLE

The Hoover Dam, Nevada, USA

The Hoover Dam has several different purposes:

- **Controlling the flow of the river**
- **Water storage**
- **HEP**
- **Recreation**
- **Tourism**

EXAMPLE

Culverts mean that river channels carry water away from areas that are at risk from flooding quickly.

Flood Control — Soft Engineering

To avoid the disadvantages of hard engineering, water authorities are moving to more sustainable flood controls, using 'soft engineering'. Instead of trying to control rivers, soft engineering works by using natural drainage basin processes to reduce flooding.

Prediction — Spotting Problems Before they Happen

Soft engineering relies on <u>detailed research</u> into drainage basin systems to work out how to solve one flood problem without causing new ones. To find out if an area is in danger of flooding, the <u>whole</u> drainage basin is looked at. Scientists assess the <u>geology</u>, <u>soil</u>, <u>drainage</u> and <u>precipitation</u> characteristics of the drainage basin.

They also investigate the <u>human activities</u> in the basin to make sure they've got a good overview of all the factors which affect channel flow in the basin. Another way of finding out when floods are likely to happen is to look for patterns in the <u>flood-history data</u> for the river.

EXAM TIP

Remember soft engineering is really popular in geography at the moment because it is more <u>sustainable</u> than hard engineering. It's worth learning because it comes up in the coasts section as well (see next page).

Changing Land Use can help Reduce Flooding

One of the easiest 'soft engineering' ways of avoiding flood problems is not to build houses where it floods. But many people already live in <u>flood zones</u> and they're not leaving, so different strategies are needed.

<u>Afforestation</u> of bare slopes in the <u>upper reaches</u> reduces run-off as trees <u>intercept</u> the rain. <u>Lag time</u> is <u>longer</u> — with <u>less</u> run-off or river discharge.

Leaving land upstream as <u>pasture</u> gives <u>continuous</u> plant cover, which reduces run-off as more water is intercepted by plants. It's better than using land for growing crops, which leaves soil bare and open to run-off during the non-growing season.

<u>Man-made</u> surfaces, such as concrete, allow <u>rapid run-off</u>. <u>Plants</u> and <u>grass</u> <u>areas</u> can be used <u>instead</u> to reduce flooding in urban areas.

<u>Traditional man-made drainage systems</u> use fast draining pipes leading directly into watercourses causing floods. <u>Sustainable Urban Drainage Systems (SUDS)</u> reduce the flow and amount of urban drainage by directing rainwater into the soil, slow draining channels or ponds.

Afforestation

Pasture land

Plants and grass areas in towns

Sustainable Urban Drainage Systems (SUDS)

Soft engineering methods

FACT

LEDCs are lagging behind — soft engineering is mostly used in MEDCs where there's more money available to invest in flood prediction, prevention and control.

Things Aren't Getting any Better

Scientists believe that the severe flooding we've had in recent years could be an effect of <u>global warming</u>. If this is true, flood control will be even more important in the future.

Flooding could become more common

TIP

See page 33 for more about global warming.

Coastal Flood and Erosion Control

There are two different approaches to defending against coastal erosion and flooding — <u>hard</u> and <u>soft</u> engineering.

There are Five main Hard Engineering Defences

- <u>Groynes</u> are wooden structures placed at right angles to the coast where longshore drift occurs. They <u>reduce</u> movement of material along the coast, and <u>hold</u> the beach in place — <u>protecting</u> the cliff from further erosion in some parts. The beach will then <u>protect</u> low areas from <u>flooding</u>.

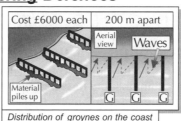

Distribution of groynes on the coast

EXAMPLES

Groynes
Bournemouth

Sea wall
Scarborough

Armour blocks
Barton-on-Sea

- <u>Sea walls</u> reduce erosion — but they <u>deflect</u> (not absorb) waves so waves can still <u>wash away</u> the protective beach. The waves also <u>erode</u> the wall itself which can collapse. Sea walls <u>protect</u> against <u>floods</u> in lowland coasts.

- <u>Revetments</u> (slatted barriers) are built where a sea wall would be <u>too expensive</u>, e.g. out of towns. They <u>break</u> the wave force, trapping beach material behind them and <u>protecting</u> the cliff base — they're <u>cheaper</u> than sea walls but look ugly and <u>don't</u> give full protection.

- <u>Gabions</u> are steel mesh cages containing boulders, built onto the cliff face above a sea wall. The rocks <u>absorb</u> some of the wave energy and <u>cut down</u> erosion — they're cheap but unattractive.

- <u>Armour blocks</u> are large boulders piled on beaches where erosion is likely. They're cheap but ugly and they can be <u>undermined</u> or <u>moved by waves</u>.

These <u>hard engineering</u> style sea defences are <u>not sustainable</u> in the long-term. They are extremely <u>expensive</u>, <u>ugly</u>, need constant <u>maintenance</u> and often cause <u>problems</u> further down the coast.

A More Sustainable Approach — Soft Engineering

The easiest <u>soft engineering</u> option is to leave the sea to do what it wants. The problem is that without control, the sea would <u>destroy</u> a lot of land by <u>floods</u> and <u>erosion</u>. Soft engineering approaches try to fit in with <u>natural</u> coastal processes and <u>protect habitats</u>.

- <u>Beach nourishment</u> — This simply means putting more pebbles or sand on the beach. The beach is an excellent natural <u>flood</u> defence, so by replacing all the sediment that's eroded, you avoid a big flood problem. The beach also prevents cliffs from being <u>eroded</u> by powerful waves. The problem is how to get the sediment without causing <u>environmental damage</u> somewhere else. It's also <u>expensive</u> and needs to be done again and again.

- <u>Shoreline vegetation</u> — Planting things like <u>marshbeds</u> on the shoreline <u>binds</u> the beach sediment together, slowing erosion. This also encourages shoreline <u>habitats</u> to develop.

- <u>Dune stabilisation</u> — Dunes are an excellent defence against <u>storm floods</u>. Sediment is added and erosion is <u>reduced</u> by footpath control and <u>marram grass</u> planting, which supports the dune ecosystem.

Dunes are good sea defences

KEY TERM

Soft engineering is based round the idea of <u>managed retreat</u> — this is slowing coastal erosion but not trying to stop it. Eventually buildings will have to be moved or lost to the sea, but this can often be cheaper than investing in constant coastal control.

- <u>Set backs</u> — Building houses set back from the coast.

Controlling Desertification

The causes of desertification are explained on page 38.
This page tells you how scientists predict where desertification will
happen and the methods that are used to try and stop it spreading.

In the <u>Sahel</u>, <u>Desertification</u> is a Big Problem

WORLD LOCATION

Sahel Region

The Sahel area in Africa experienced a number of severe <u>droughts</u> during the
1970s and 80s. During this period the Sahara desert expanded southwards
reducing the amount of fertile farmland. It is thought that about
<u>1 million people</u> died during the droughts.

Millions of people live in the area and the encroaching desert means that they
can't grow enough food to feed their families because <u>yields</u> have decreased.
Also there is little wood left for them to use as <u>fuel</u>, and the poor growing
conditions mean that it is difficult to grow new trees to provide fuel in the future.

<u>Remote Sensing</u> is Used To <u>Predict Desertification</u>

SAHEL LOCATION

Africa

□ Area of severe
desertification

1 Niger 4 Ethiopia
2 Chad 5 Somalia
3 Sudan

Remote sensing uses sensors attached to <u>planes</u> and <u>satellites</u> to collect
information about the Earth. This information is analysed by <u>computers</u> to show
changes or trends in environmental processes. Remote sensing can be used to
monitor <u>large areas</u>, which makes it ideal for studying the Sahel region.

In the Sahel, remote sensing is used to assess how much <u>vegetation cover</u> there is
and changes in the <u>ocean temperatures</u> of the Atlantic and the Indian Oceans.
Changes in the temperatures can indicate that a <u>drought</u> period is likely.

<u>Desertification</u> can be <u>Controlled</u> and Possibly <u>Reduced</u>

TIP

Shelter belts are often
planted using
perennials (plants that
live from year to year)
so that the soil is held
together by their roots
all the time.

Many different methods are used to try and stop desertification. If these methods
are used in combination then areas which have suffered from desertification can
even begin to <u>recover</u>. The methods used include:

- Planting 'shelter belts' of vegetation between the grassland and the desert.
- <u>Terracing</u> hill slopes to reduce soil run-off and increase soil moisture storage.
- Using <u>branches</u> rather than whole trees for <u>fuel</u>.
- Using land <u>less intensively</u> and enabling it to <u>recover</u> every couple of years.
- <u>Political efforts</u> to solve wider problems associated with desertification like
  civil wars, overpopulation and intensive farming would help in the <u>long-term</u>.

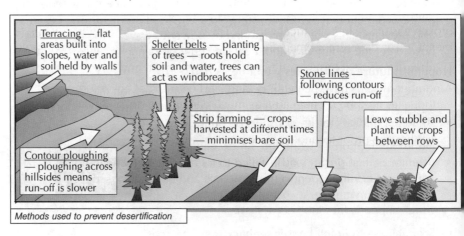

Methods used to prevent desertification

Case Studies

For the exam you need to know some examples of how people are trying to predict hazards and reduce their impacts.

Case Study 1: *Controlling the Mississippi River, USA*

The Mississippi river system drains <u>one third</u> of the land in the <u>USA</u> and a small area in <u>Canada</u>. The <u>Ohio</u>, <u>Tennessee</u> and <u>Missouri Rivers</u> are the main <u>tributaries</u> of the Mississippi. The river naturally <u>floods</u> frequently, especially when the snow in the <u>Appalachian Mountains</u> melts and flows into the river. The areas worst affected by the flooding are the towns below St. Louis in the lower section of the basin.

WORLD LOCATION

Mississippi Basin

Hard engineering has been used to protect the floodplain:

Following a major flood in 1927, the <u>US Army Corps of Engineers</u> used hard engineering to prevent flooding:

- <u>Levees</u> were built along the river banks to contain the increased discharge.

- The channel was <u>straightened</u> to make the water flow to the sea more quickly.

- <u>Dams</u> were built on the Missouri and the Tennessee to control the amount of water flowing through the basin.

After these methods were introduced there was very little flooding for a while and people thought that the river was under control.

In <u>1993</u> there was another big flood:

In 1993 the Mississippi flooded <u>severely</u>. The flood caused <u>45 deaths</u> and damage costing <u>US$ 11 billion</u>. The flood waters broke through the levees and spread through urban areas and across farmland.

The 1993 flood made a lot of people cease to trust the hard engineering strategies. It seemed obvious that the river can never be properly <u>controlled</u> by people. So more recently soft engineering strategies, including <u>afforestation</u> schemes, have been employed, to try and fit in with the natural river system.

USA LOCATION

Case Study 2: *Earthquake in Kobe, Japan in 1995*

<u>Kobe</u> is a city in Japan that's close to the margin of three <u>tectonic plates</u>. In 1995 there was an earthquake measuring <u>7.2</u> on the Richter scale. The epicentre was under the sea in <u>Osaka Bay</u>.

Over <u>5000 people</u> were killed and thousands injured. Many buildings, including schools, <u>collapsed</u>, and roads and railways were damaged. Lots of fires started because of

Damaged road systems in Kobe

WORLD LOCATION

Japan

broken gas pipes and electrical cables. The damage to the <u>transport systems</u> meant it was difficult for emergency services to access the fires and the injured.

Hopefully, future earthquakes won't be as bad:

A number of steps have been taken to try and ensure that any future earthquakes in Kobe do not cause as much damage, injury and death:

- All new buildings in the city must be built using <u>earthquake-proof technology</u> (see page 41).

- <u>Monitoring equipment</u> was installed to try and <u>predict</u> when future earthquakes will happen so that residents and emergency services can be given warning.

- A new <u>emergency plan</u> has been made so there will be a more <u>organised response</u> if there is another earthquake.

JAPANESE LOCATION

Japan
Kobe · Tokyo

Revision Summary

This section is all about how the effects of natural hazards can be reduced. Sometimes people can take direct action to prevent them (like afforestation), but at other times predicting hazards and being prepared to deal with them is the best way to prevent a disaster (like droughts). Have a go at these questions and keep trying them until you can answer them all. If you're struggling, go back over section four, about how these hazards are caused, and relate it to predicting and preventing hazards.

1) Make a table which shows the advantages and disadvantages of living in areas where there are earthquakes and volcanoes.

2) What signs do scientists look for when they're trying to predict a volcanic eruption?

3) How do 'earthquake-proof' buildings work?

4) Name three factors which determine how serious the effects of a hazard are.

5) Write a mini-essay explaining why MEDCs can cope with natural hazards better than LEDCs.

6) What are the purposes of the Hoover dam?

7) What problems can dams cause in terms of sediment flow?

8) What is a culvert?

9) What is the difference between 'hard' and 'soft' engineering?

10) Why is soft engineering popular in geography at the moment?

11) Why does increasing the number of impermeable surfaces in an area increase the likelihood of flooding?

12) How do groynes work? Name a place where they are used.

13) What are gabions?

14) Name a place where armour blocks are used.

15) Name three soft engineering methods of protecting coasts.

16) Why is remote sensing useful for monitoring desertification?

17) Write a paragraph to explain methods that can be used to reduce desertification.

18) Draw a location map to show the Sahel area.

19) Draw a location map of the Mississippi drainage basin.

20) Name the three major tributaries of the Mississippi.

21) What flood protection methods have been used on the Mississippi?

22) What were the consequences of the 1993 Mississippi flood?

23) Write a short paragraph explaining how you think the Mississippi should be managed in the future.

24) When was the Kobe earthquake?

25) How many people were killed in the Kobe earthquake?

26) Name three steps that have been taken to reduce the damage caused by future earthquakes in Kobe.

TIP

It doesn't really matter if you don't understand the science behind remote sensing. All you need to be able to do is say what it is used for and why it is useful.

Classification of Industry

There are <u>four types</u> of industry — they are classified according to the processes that take place.

Primary Industry Involves Collecting <u>Raw Materials</u>

<u>Raw materials</u> are anything <u>naturally present</u> in or on the earth <u>before</u> processing. They are collected in three ways:

- They can be <u>quarried</u>, <u>mined</u> or <u>drilled for</u> below the Earth's surface — e.g. coal mining and oil drilling.

- They can be <u>grown</u> — e.g. farming and forestry.

- They can be <u>collected</u> from the sea — e.g. fishing.

Primary Industry

Secondary Industry is Manufacturing a <u>Product</u>

A secondary industry is where a product from primary industry is turned into <u>another product</u>.

The <u>finished product</u> of one secondary industry may be <u>raw material</u> for another, e.g. one factory may make tyres which are then sent on to be used in a car plant.

Secondary Industry

EXAMPLES

Types of industry

Primary	Farmer grows potatoes
Secondary	Factory processes potatoes into crisps
Tertiary	Shopkeeper sells crisps
Quaternary	Scientists research new production methods

Tertiary Industry Provides a <u>Service</u>

Tertiary Industry

Tertiary industry is the <u>largest</u> group of industries in <u>MEDCs</u>. It involves a wide range of services — anything from teaching, nursing and retailing to the police force or the civil service and transport.

Quaternary Industry Involves <u>Research</u> and <u>Development</u>

Quaternary industry is where scientists and researchers investigate and develop new products to sell.

Quaternary industry is the <u>newest</u> and smallest industrial sector, but it's growing rapidly due to developments in <u>information technology</u> and <u>communication</u>.

Quaternary Industry

EXAM TIP

Think of some examples of the different types of industry. Try to put them into a chain like the examples above. Remember, quaternary industry is less common than the others — it doesn't have to be part of the process unless the company needs new research.

Industry is <u>Not</u> the Same as <u>Employment</u>

<u>Industry</u> is part of a <u>chain</u> — from raw materials to finished product, finished product to service sector and service sector to research and development.

<u>Employment</u> is the <u>job</u> you do. So you could have a tertiary job as a secretary in a secondary industry like a toy factory.

Industry as a System

For the exam, you need to be able to describe the features of the factory system, and the factors that affect them.

The <u>Factory System</u> has <u>Inputs</u>, <u>Processes</u> and <u>Outputs</u>

<u>Inputs</u> are the items that go into making a product. These can be the <u>raw materials</u> themselves, but also include <u>investment capital</u>, <u>labour</u>, <u>buildings</u> and <u>machinery</u> — anything needed before the production process can take place.

<u>Processes</u> are factory activities that transform raw materials into the finished product. This includes not only the <u>physical manufacture</u> of the product, but all the <u>support services</u> such as design and packaging — everything needed to make the product.

<u>Outputs</u> are what comes out of the factory after the production process. This includes a <u>finished product</u> and <u>by-products</u> (secondary products made during the processing of the main product), <u>waste</u> and hopefully <u>profit</u>.

The diagram below shows an example of how inputs, processes and outputs fit together for a shirt factory.

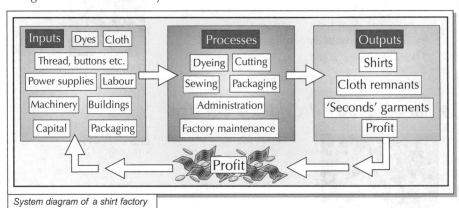

System diagram of a shirt factory

<u>Linkage</u> is when <u>One Industry</u> Depends on the <u>Output</u> of Another

Linkage causes problems if one industry has production problems or closes down <u>The car industry</u> is a good example — each part labelled on the diagram below may be produced by a <u>different company</u> before it goes to the <u>assembly plant</u>.

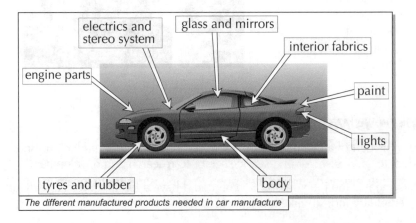

The different manufactured products needed in car manufacture

Location of Industry

The growth of cities, population distribution and social and employment changes have all been affected by the location of industry. This page and the next page describe the <u>four</u> big influences on the location of industry — <u>raw materials</u>, <u>labour supply</u>, <u>transport</u> and <u>the market</u>.

Raw Materials Influence *Industrial Location*

During the Industrial Revolution, new industries needed <u>power supplies</u> (originally fast-flowing streams) and <u>raw materials</u> such as coal or iron ore. Industry grew up where these were easily available.

A pattern of industrial location developed where different areas specialised in industries using <u>local resources</u>. As most of our natural resources are in the <u>north of England</u>, this became our <u>industrial heartland</u>.

Location <u>near</u> raw materials reduces <u>transport costs</u>, particularly if they are bulky or lose weight during the manufacturing process.

<u>Ports</u> became important too, as they were the source of <u>imported</u> raw materials.

EXAMPLES
Locations of industry:
Local resources South Wales — coal Sheffield — steel (particularly cutlery) Newcastle — ship building
Ports Liverpool, Bristol

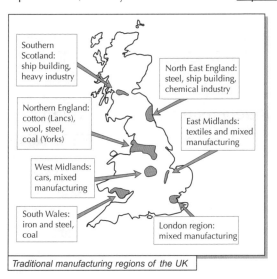

Traditional manufacturing regions of the UK

Labour Supply has Influenced *Industrial Location*

<u>Availability of labour supply</u> is important to industry. A factory is likely to locate where there are enough people looking for work to fill their needs. Unemployment varies enormously by region, so this can be an important factor. The labour supply must be <u>suitable</u>. There are three main types of labour requirement:

EXAMPLES	
Labour requirements	
Unskilled labour	Processed food manufacturer
Specialised workforce	Car manufacturer
Highly skilled workforce	Scientific research laboratories

- A large pool of <u>unskilled labour</u> — some industries will <u>train</u> their own workforce in the necessary skills, and simply need a large group of <u>available people</u>.

- A large <u>specialised workforce</u> — some industries need a large workforce with particular <u>skills</u>, and they will often locate near <u>similar industries</u>, as the workforce will meet this requirement.

- A small <u>highly skilled workforce</u> — some industries need <u>highly skilled</u> or <u>qualified</u> staff, and will need to locate where these people are <u>available</u>.

Labour <u>costs</u> also vary around the country, so industries try to locate in an area where they can keep these costs down. Industries requiring highly skilled workers are <u>less likely</u> to be able to do this.

Location of Industry

This page covers more factors that affect the location of industry.

Transport Influences Location in Three Ways

The cost of transporting raw materials and finished product:
If the raw materials cost more to transport than the finished product
(they may produce a lot of waste during manufacture, for instance)
it is cheaper to locate near the raw materials.

If the finished product is more expensive to transport (it may take up more space,
or be expensive to insure) then the cheaper location will be nearer the market.

The type of transport used:
Traditionally, bulky cargo was transported by rail, so rail links were important.
The increase in road transport in recent years has changed this. Many industries
are now located near main roads, particularly motorway intersections.
Small high value items can be transported by air, but this is expensive.
Goods destined for overseas markets are transported by ship, often using
container lorries and roll-on roll-off ferries.

The speed required:
Some products need to be transported quickly, possibly because they go off
quickly (e.g. milk). This may require a more expensive form of transport.

The Market Influences Industrial Location

The market is where a product is sold —
usually a lot of separate places.

Location near the market is best when
transporting the product is expensive.
For some UK industries who export to
Europe, a location in southern England
has become attractive.

When products are sent on from one
industry to another it helps to be
located close by. This leads to
industrial agglomeration.

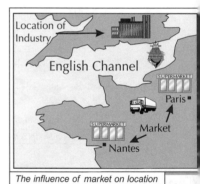

The influence of market on location

An agglomeration needs lots of labour in the region.
A skilled labour force attracts more industries to the area.
This means that labour pools and markets are often found in the same place.

Other Factors Influence Industrial Location too

Some industries are heavily reliant on large amounts of energy. These industries
should be close to the energy source, or in a suitable location to receive imports.

Finance affects the location of industry — the cost of land varies from
place to place. Also, more capital is needed for the larger industries.

Physical site affects the location of industry because some types of industry
need particular sites, e.g. large factories need to be built on large, flat areas.

Another important factor is government policy. The government will
encourage certain types of industry according to the social and
economic conditions at the time.

The Farm as a System

Agriculture and food production are basic to any society. The ability of a country to feed its people is fundamental to developing its industry.

A Farm System — *Inputs*, *Processes* and *Outputs*

A farm can be a system in much the same way as a factory can.

It has the added element of the farmer as a decision maker who has to deal with a huge array of inputs. The farmer's role is shown in the diagram below — his or her decisions affect the processes.

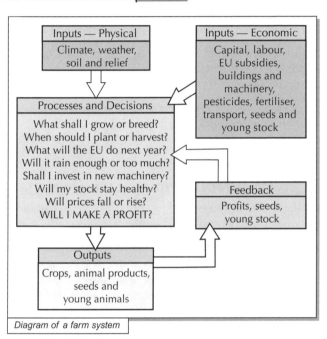

Diagram of a farm system

> **EXAM TIP**
>
> Remember — farming is an example of a **primary industry** (see page 49).

A Farmer's Job is *Unpredictable*

Farmers have to make decisions which rely on factors beyond their control, e.g. the weather. These things determine whether they make a profit or a loss.

Government and European Union (EU) policy will also affect decisions made, and can change at any time. This can be a problem for farmers who have to plan several years in advance.

Farmers depend on the prices they can get for their produce, both locally and on a global scale. These vary from year to year — if the harvest is good, there can be a glut (too much) of a product, and prices will fall; if the harvest is poor, prices will rise, but the farmer has little to sell.

Farmers Have to Deal with *Hazards*

Expensive animals can become sick at any time, and a farmer could lose his entire stock. Climatic hazards such as drought or flood also affect farmers, and pests such as locusts can reduce a harvest to almost nothing in a short time.

Farmers decide what levels of pesticides or fertilisers to use on their land. They must balance the need for a high yield against safety and consumer preference (i.e. what customers want).

> **EXAMPLE**
>
> The 2001 outbreak of foot and mouth disease in the UK led to the loss of livestock for hundreds of farmers.

Distribution of Farming Types

Farming depends on the physical characteristics of an area —
the climate, soils and relief. Different farming types are
associated with different areas, on a global and regional scale.

The Farming Type Depends on the Climate

On a global scale, patterns of farming are associated with climatic belts —
with distinct differences between the temperate and tropical climatic zones.

The temperate latitudes have mainly commercial farming — most of the
countries involved are MEDCs — and their produce includes cereals,
livestock and mixed farming. Intensive and extensive farming are found here.

The tropical latitudes have both commercial and subsistence farming,
and mostly include LEDCs. Plantations are also important in tropical areas,
e.g. tea and cocoa beans.

Areas of extreme climate (either hot or cold) have little sedentary (fixed)
farming, but nomadic hunters or herders are found.

Rainfall and Relief Affect Farming on a Regional Scale

Patterns of farming can be identified within countries due to variations in rainfall
and relief — the causes are demonstrated by the patterns evident in the UK:

Western UK receives more relief rainfall due to its upland areas and prevailing
westerly winds — the east has less rainfall, is flatter, and has a longer growing
season. Farms in the south and east are more intensive, have larger fields
and use more machinery than those in the north and west. This results in
the distribution shown below. Remember that there are more types of farming
in the UK than this, but there is a clear general pattern by region.

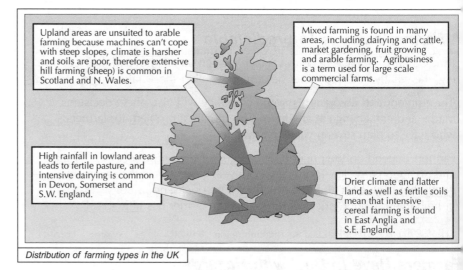

Upland areas are unsuited to arable
farming because machines can't cope
with steep slopes, climate is harsher
and soils are poor, therefore extensive
hill farming (sheep) is common in
Scotland and N. Wales.

Mixed farming is found in many
areas, including dairying and cattle,
market gardening, fruit growing
and arable farming. Agribusiness
is a term used for large scale
commercial farms.

High rainfall in lowland areas
leads to fertile pasture, and
intensive dairying is common
in Devon, Somerset and
S.W. England.

Drier climate and flatter
land as well as fertile soils
mean that intensive
cereal farming is found
in East Anglia and
S.E. England.

Distribution of farming types in the UK

Economic and Political Issues also Affect Farming

Physical characteristics are not the only influence on farming types, but they
do dictate what type of farming is possible. Economic and political influences
are also important, e.g. nearness to market and government quotas.

You've got to know a case study of industry as a system. This includes inputs, processes and outputs, and the reasons why the industry located where it did.

Case Study — <u>*Nissan Motor Corporation, Washington*</u>

<u>Nissan</u> is a <u>Japanese</u> car firm with an <u>assembly plant</u> in Washington near Sunderland in north east England. Historically, Washington relied on <u>heavy industry</u> for employment. When these industries closed down the economy in the area declined a lot and there was high unemployment.

To improve the local economy, the government gave the Nissan corporation a <u>grant</u> to locate in Washington. However, that wasn't the only reason why it located there.

Lots of factors made Washington <u>attractive</u> to Nissan:

- There are <u>good communication links</u> to the rest of the UK and EU: The A1(M) and the A19 are major roads which connect the north east with the rest of the British mainland. There are good port facilities for exporting goods at Teesport which is only 20 miles from Washington. There are also good air and rail links so visitors and staff can get to the plant easily.

- There was a <u>greenfield site</u> available next to the A19 with space for expansion meaning that Nissan could build a factory to meet their needs.

- A <u>skilled work force</u> live nearby in Washington, Sunderland, Middlesbrough, Gateshead and Newcastle-upon-Tyne. The high unemployment meant that enough people would be looking for work to staff the plant.

- The <u>wage costs</u> for labour are <u>cheaper</u> than Japan.

- Cars made in the EU do not have <u>import restrictions</u>. The EU has 360 million people, which is a large market for Nissan to sell to.

- <u>Steel</u> for the cars is supplied by <u>Corus</u> (formerly British Steel). Corus are based nearby on Teesside so the transport costs for inputs are cheap.

- <u>Universities</u> in the area are involved in industrial <u>research</u> so Nissan can work with academics to develop more efficient machinery.

The car industry works as a <u>system</u>

The Nissan plant is the most efficient in Europe — each employee produces 100 cars per year. The plant is a system with <u>inputs, processes and outputs</u>:

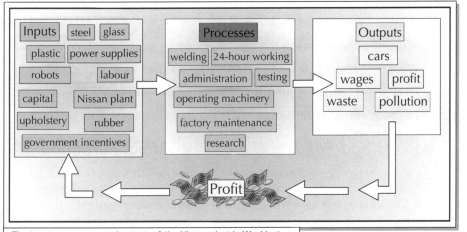

The inputs, processes and outputs of the Nissan plant in Washington

UK LOCATION

Washington

KEY TERM

The Nissan plant uses a kind of production called <u>just-in-time</u>. This means that all the cars are made to order. Parts are ordered in when they are needed instead of being stored just in case they are needed. Just-in-time production is popular because it minimises waste and makes the system more efficient.

FACT

The Nissan plant has had a positive effect on the local economy. Other firms which supply goods to the factory have moved to the north east. For example SP Tyres have located nearby to reduce the cost of delivering goods to the Nissan factory.

Revision Summary

This section's a short one, so there's not too much to worry about. Just make sure you have a go at the questions on this page, and then you'll have an idea of how much more revision you need to do. Keep looking back over the section and revising it until you can answer all of these questions, no problem.

1) Give four examples of primary industry.

2) How is secondary industry different to primary industry?

3) Which of the four types of industry is the largest in MEDCs?

4) Which is the newest type of industry? Why is it growing rapidly?

5) Name three things that might be classed as inputs in the factory system.

6) Write the definitions of processes and outputs. Give an example of each.

7) Draw a simple systems diagram for a factory of your choice.

8) What is linkage?

9) Why did industry grow up where it did during the Industrial Revolution?

10) Name the types of manufacturing that traditionally happened in
a) North-East England   b) South Wales and   c) the West Midlands.

11) List the three main types of labour requirement.
Which type of industry might need which type of labour?

12) Are industries requiring highly skilled workers likely to be able to locate in places where they can keep costs down?

13) How has the location of industry changed due to transport developments?

14) List an advantage and a disadvantage for rail, air, road and sea transport.

15) What is an industrial agglomeration? How would one happen?

16) Name three other factors which might affect the location of industry.

17) Name three physical inputs to the farm system.

18) Give an example of a decision a farmer might have to make.

19) What makes a farmer's job unpredictable?

20) Name one hazard which caused a massive problem for farmers in the past.

21) Give an example of farming in   a) a temperate climate
b) a tropical climate   c) an extreme climate.

22) Which type of farming is the most common in south-east England and why?

23) Which type of farming is the most common in upland areas? Why is this?

24) What might affect the type of farming apart from physical characteristics?

25) Draw a sketch map of the UK and show where Washington is.

26) Describe seven factors which made Washington attractive to Nissan.

27) Draw a table to list the inputs, processes and outputs of the Nissan factory.

KEY TERM

In this section, there are lots of maps and diagrams. Don't just ignore them — they're not there for decoration. Make sure you learn all the points in them in the same way you'd learn anything else.

Changing Industry — MEDCs

Industry in MEDCs has changed a lot in the last 50 years for a variety of reasons.

Traditional Manufacturing has Declined and the _Service Sector_ has Grown

Raw materials have started to run out:
Many natural resources have been used up and others are too expensive to continue extracting. Some materials are now imported from abroad.

Competition from other countries has increased:
Many LEDCs manufacture goods at cheaper costs than MEDCs can. This is often due to lower wages and poorer working conditions as well as less strict pollution controls.

> **EXAMPLE**
>
> **The coal belt across the Midlands has been exhausted. This means that the coal mining industry no longer exists in the area (e.g. in Derbyshire and Staffordshire).**

This has _Two Effects_ on Industrial Location

Many industries have relocated near ports where raw materials are imported.

New tertiary industries are often footloose, meaning they are not tied to a raw material location, and locate in pleasant environments near transport routes and near the markets (e.g. hi-tech industries like computing).

> **EXAMPLE**
>
> **Many companies (e.g. HSBC) have moved their call centres to places like Delhi in India, where running costs are cheaper.**

The _Service Sector_ is now the _Largest Employer_

Increasing mechanisation and the use of robots have led to a decline in the numbers employed in secondary industry. However, there have been increases in tertiary industries. The pie charts show the change in the UK.

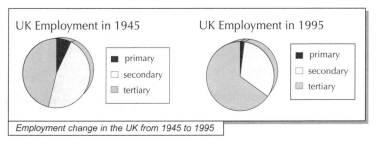

UK Employment in 1945   UK Employment in 1995

- primary
- secondary
- tertiary

Employment change in the UK from 1945 to 1995

Footloose Industries often Locate in _Science Parks_

Science parks are estates of modern, usually footloose industries such as pharmaceuticals and computing companies, which have grown up in recent years on the outskirts of towns. There are three main reasons for their growth:

- The need to be near raw materials has been replaced by the need to be near research centres like universities and similar industries. Developments in hi-tech industry happen fast so companies need to be up-to-date to survive.

- Land is often cheaper on the town outskirts than in the traditional central industrial areas, and access to transport routes is better.

- Information technology is increasingly allowing hi-tech industry to locate further away from heavily populated areas. The use of faxes and e-mails, for example, mean that face-to-face contact is no longer necessary.

> **EXAMPLES**
>
> | Science parks |
> | --- |
> | Silicon Glen, Scotland |
> | Cambridge Science Park, Cambridge |

Changing Industry — LEDCs

The characteristics of industry in LEDCs are different from those in MEDCs.

Industry in an *LEDC* can be *Formal* or *Informal*

The formal sector is regular waged employment, usually manufacturing. Wages are often low and hours can be long, but it provides a regular income.

The informal sector is usually work in small scale manufacturing or service industries — where people create their own employment to meet local demand.

In many LEDCs, more people look for work in the formal sector than there are jobs. So the informal sector plays a vital role in the economy of many countries, employing more people than the formal sector.

There is little or no security in the informal sector, and many people are trapped by lack of opportunity to improve their position.

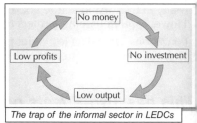

The trap of the informal sector in LEDCs

EXAMPLES	
Formal sector	Breweries Clothes manufacturers
Informal sector	Tourist Guides Shoe Cleaners Food sellers

LEDCs have found it difficult to develop their formal sector, because they don't have the money to invest in it, and lack the infrastructure (power supplies and transport networks) necessary for success. Many large companies in LEDCs are multinationals (see p. 62).

Some LEDCs are now *Newly Industrialised Countries*

Not all LEDCs share the same characteristics as those described above. Some, like the Pacific Rim countries in South East Asia and Brazil and Mexico, are a separate case.

The Pacific Rim countries have seen dramatic levels of industrialisation in the last few decades, so they're called Newly Industrialised Countries (NICs).

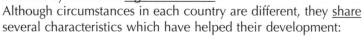

WORLD LOCATION

Pacific Rim

The greatest level of industrialisation has occurred in South Korea, Taiwan, Hong Kong and Singapore — collectively known as Tiger Economies.

The built-up skyline of Singapore

Although circumstances in each country are different, they share several characteristics which have helped their development:

- They invested in infrastructure during the 1960s.

- They have a motivated and cheap work force which attracted American and Japanese investors.

- They invested money very cleverly in new hi-tech products.

- They have a large population which is a home market for the goods.

ASIAN LOCATION

As a result, NICs like those of the Pacific Rim have become formidable competition to the manufacturing industries of MEDCs and no longer have all the characteristics associated with LEDCs.

There have been some negative consequences for the NICs. The manufacturing industry has caused a lot of air pollution. People's health can be damaged because of poor working conditions in factories. Also, relying on foreign investment means that economies are unstable when there are recessions.

Farming in the European Union (EU)

There have been significant changes in the farming industry since the <u>Common Agricultural Policy</u> (CAP) was set up.

A CAP Target is to <u>Increase</u> Farming <u>Efficiency</u>

CAP now governs farming in all countries in the EU. It was set up after World War Two to increase European food production by making farming more <u>modern</u> and <u>efficient</u>.

The CAP introduced <u>subsidies</u> (payments) to encourage farmers to produce more and become more efficient.

However, encouraging farmers to increase their yields led to <u>environmental</u> problems. There was an increase in chemical <u>fertilisers</u> and <u>pesticides</u>, which presented a threat to <u>wildlife</u>. And there are other problems:

Over <u>25%</u> of UK Hedgerows Have been <u>Removed</u> Since 1945

Farmers in arable areas use large and expensive machinery because it is more <u>efficient</u>. This has resulted in the <u>removal of hedgerows</u> for three reasons:

- Larger fields make using huge machinery easier.

- Land used for hedgerows can be brought into cultivation — increasing <u>yield</u>.

- Hedgerows take time and money to <u>maintain</u>, and harbour <u>pests</u> and <u>weeds</u>.

All these factors encouraged farmers to remove hedgerows from their fields. But concern has been increasing over this for the reasons shown in the diagram.

> **EXAMPLE**
>
> **Many hedgerows have been removed from eastern counties, such as Norfolk and Kent, where arable farming dominates.**

Hedgerows are attractive and their removal changes the character of the landscape	Hedgerows act as windbreaks and their roots hold the soil — their removal can cause soil erosion	Hedgerows provide habitats for wildlife — their removal can affect the whole food chain and put many species at risk

Problems caused by the removal of hedgerows

CAP Worked Too Well — Producing <u>Food Mountains</u>

After World War Two farmers were given <u>subsidies</u> (assistance money) to encourage them to produce <u>more</u>.

The EU guaranteed a <u>standard price</u> for farmers' products regardless of market forces or the price of the same product outside Europe — this protected the farmers from <u>cheap imports</u> from abroad.

The subsidies and guaranteed prices meant the EU farmers ended up damaging the environment and producing <u>too much food</u> — gluts of butter, grain, milk and wine — called <u>food mountains</u>. The surplus food had to be <u>stored</u> and later <u>destroyed</u> costing huge amounts of money.

> **EXAMPLE**
>
> **Many people think it is wasteful to have huge stocks of food in Europe when people in poorer parts of the world are starving. Sometimes food stocks are given to poorer regions as aid.**

Farming in the European Union (EU)

The EU tried to stop over-production and protect the environment in <u>four ways</u>:

The EU Introduced <u>Quotas</u> to Reduce <u>Milk Production</u>

The UK joined the EU in 1973. <u>Quotas</u> were imposed in 1984 to control <u>milk production</u> across Europe, limiting the amount of milk each farmer was allowed to produce.

<u>Fines</u> were set for milk produced <u>over this limit</u>, creating two difficulties:

- The quotas were based on a production level <u>below</u> the current one — so some farmers had to <u>reduce</u> their milk production.

- The quota level <u>didn't</u> take into account any <u>expansion</u> of farmers' dairy herds, so if a herd was below normal size (e.g. because of illness) the quota <u>lowered</u> the production level automatically. When the herd <u>grew</u>, the farm would <u>overproduce</u>.

<u>Set-Aside</u> was Introduced to Reduce <u>Food Production</u>

<u>Set-aside</u> means the EU pays farmers a <u>subsidy</u> to leave land <u>uncultivated</u> to reduce overall production. It began as a <u>voluntary</u> scheme in 1988, but by 1992 there was still a <u>surplus</u> of cereals being produced.

In order to continue receiving EU <u>subsidies</u>, all farms with over 20 hectares of land must now leave <u>15%</u> of it as <u>set-aside</u>. It should be left for at least <u>five years</u>, and though they cannot farm it, they can use it for <u>other purposes</u>.

<u>Diversification Schemes</u> Use Farmland for Other Things

<u>Diversification</u> is when farmers develop other <u>business activities</u> in addition to their <u>traditional ones</u>. The aim of farm diversification is to:

- Reduce farm surpluses — to prevent <u>food mountains</u>.

- Cater for the increased <u>demand</u> for <u>leisure activities</u> in rural areas.

- Reduce the <u>damage</u> to the environment caused by modern farming.

In addition to traditional farming duties, nowadays farms often provide other services and leisure opportunities to boost their income:

Farm land uses

- <u>Rare breeds</u>, <u>specialist centres</u> and <u>pets' corners</u>

- <u>Adventure playgrounds</u> and <u>nature trails</u>.

- <u>Tea</u> shops and <u>craft</u> shops.

- <u>Bed and breakfast</u> and holiday <u>accommodation</u>

- <u>Pony trekking</u> and <u>horse riding</u>.

- <u>Hobby farming</u> is a term for <u>specialist farms</u> centred around the farmer's interest (e.g. a rare breed or plant) — these have potential as <u>visitor centres</u> and can broaden the farmer's income.

<u>ESAs</u> were Set Up

<u>Environmentally sensitive areas</u> (ESAs) were set up in the early 1990s as a result of increasing pressure by conservationists to protect the environment.

Farmers in these areas can obtain <u>subsidies</u> if they farm in an '<u>environmentally friendly</u>' way. This means things like using <u>organic</u> farming with traditional farming methods — using horses instead of tractors, using manure and not chemicals, using dry-stone walls and hedgerows.

Economic Growth and Decline

Economic activity constantly changes over time in different regions and countries. Economies grow or decline depending on a number of different factors like technology, government investment, competition and market trends.

Technology has Vastly Improved

The use of technology has allowed changes in industrial location. With improved communications and the use of technology, it isn't necessary to locate close to energy supplies, the market or other businesses. Businesses can be part of a global industrial community without a specific location. Businesses that can't afford to buy into new technologies will be at a disadvantage because they will not be able to compete with those who can afford the technology.

Mechanised car production

> **TIP**
>
> The use of machinery has led to some job losses because machines can now do the jobs that people did in the past. Businesses prefer to use machines because they can operate 24 hours a day. Machines are often faster than people and they don't take holidays or time off due to illness.

Investing in technology has had a positive impact in many LEDCs. It has caused significant improvements in their secondary and tertiary industries and therefore an increase in job opportunities. Investment has also led to the development of some LEDCs into newly industrialised countries (see p.58).

For example, India has established a National Information Technology Task Force. The Indian government encourages the development of technology companies by giving them tax relief. Indian exports of software are thriving and many service industries using IT now use India as a base.

Government Investment can Improve Areas of Decline

Governments can choose to spend money on specific areas of a country that are suffering from industrial decline and unemployment. Both the UK government and the EU have regional policies to give financial assistance to areas where there is serious industrial decline.

Nissan car plant in Washington

For example, the British government gave the Nissan car company a grant to locate in Washington in north east England, an area of industrial decline. Local people who had suffered job losses from traditional industries had the opportunity to work again, which brought money into the local economy. This increased money attracted other businesses to the area so there was an overall growth in the local economy. (See page 55 for more on the Washington Nissan plant.)

UK LOCATION
Washington

Competition from Other Areas can Lead to Decline

Competition from overseas can cause economic change in an area. For example, in south Wales many of the coal mines have closed because coal imported from abroad is cheaper than Welsh coal. The closure of the coal mines has caused wider economic decline across the region.

Market Trends Have Big Effects on Industries

If demand for a product or service falls, then industries that produce it are likely to decline. On the other hand, if a product becomes very fashionable (like mobile phones) or very popular (like garden furniture during a heat wave) the demand for it will increase and the industry which makes it will experience growth.

Multinationals

Multinationals or MNCs (multi-national companies) are large corporations with branches in several countries. They've grown huge in trade and manufacturing over the last thirty years. Sometimes they're also called Transnational companies or TNCs.

Multinationals are Vital for World Manufacturing

Multinationals place different parts of their company in locations with the greatest benefits. The headquarters and Research and Development (R & D) are usually located in MEDCs where research facilities and staff expertise are better. The manufacturing process is often completed in LEDCs or NICs where wages are lower, so production costs are cheaper.

Multinationals are extremely powerful. The largest — oil companies and car makers — have an annual turnover greater than the Gross National Product (GNP) (see page 70) of many LEDCs. It's estimated that in 1990 the hundred top multinationals controlled around 50% of all world manufacturing.

Many LEDCs try to attract multinationals by offering few restrictions on them, because they bring important capital investment into the country. This lack of restriction makes the multinationals even more powerful.

In the past, European and American companies controlled the global economy, but now the Asian companies are becoming dominant. In 1972 there was one Japanese firm in the UK — by 1991 there were 220.

The UK motorcycle industry was put out of business altogether at one stage, due to competition from Japan. Competition from NICs is also growing.

EXAMPLE

The Coca-Cola MNC:

HQ	Atlanta, USA
Sold and made	In over 200 countries
Annual revenue	US$ 21 billion
Drunk by	A billion people every day.

EXAMPLE

Companies like the Malaysian car firm Proton are increasing their share of the European car market.

There are Advantages and Disadvantages for Countries where MNCs Operate

Advantages	Disadvantages
Multinationals:	Multinationals:
provide jobs and training for local people.	provide mostly low paid jobs often with long hours.
bring investment to the country.	bring in foreign nationals for management and higher paid positions.
provide expensive machinery and equipment which the host country cannot afford.	take much of the profit out of the host country.
increase international trade and bring foreign currency.	make products for export rather than for the domestic market.
provide health care and education for their workers and families.	can pull out of the host country at any time — the host may become dependent on their employment.
increase wealth, providing a domestic market for consumer goods — which then creates more industry.	may pay little regard to the protection of the host country's environment.

The advantages and disadvantages of investment in countries by MNCs

EXAM TIP

The information in the table provides a good basis for answering loads of different questions about MNCs.

The Problems of Transport

Developing industry means developing a <u>transport system</u> — they go hand in hand.

Congestion is a Problem in <u>MEDC Urban Areas</u>

<u>Congestion</u> is a common problem because of the increased <u>number of vehicles</u> on the roads in the last few decades. There are two main reasons for this increase:

- <u>Car ownership has increased</u> — lots of households own more than one car, and many companies provide cars for their employees.

- <u>Freight</u> is now transported by <u>road</u> rather than <u>rail</u>, especially since the introduction of <u>specialist container lorries</u> (like refrigerated lorries).

The time people spend in traffic jams going to and from work means <u>increased pollution</u> and <u>lost work-time</u> for industries like delivery companies. This is bad for business and therefore bad for the economy. Many large cities have developed <u>traffic strategies</u> for dealing with this:

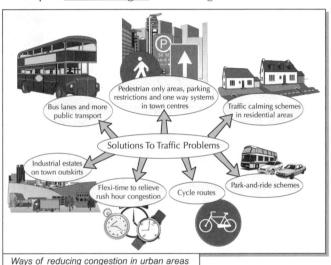

Ways of reducing congestion in urban areas

Building New Roads can Cause <u>Environmental Problems</u>

- <u>Wildlife habitats</u> are <u>destroyed</u> by the building of roads and the arrival of new industrial estates which are attracted to the new road network.

- New roads encourage <u>more vehicles</u>, which means more <u>air pollution</u>, <u>noise</u> and <u>congestion</u>.

Poor Transport Routes are a Problem in <u>LEDCs</u>

- Many <u>LEDCs</u> have problems transporting <u>goods</u> and <u>people</u> due to <u>poor roads</u>. This causes major problems for the <u>development of industry</u>, and helps to explain why <u>new</u> development in LEDCs is often near <u>ports</u>, where the goods can be exported easily.

- These problems can be made worse by <u>hot or wet climates</u>, where roads are either <u>washed away</u>, become full of pot holes or become <u>too dry</u> and dusty.

- Countries with <u>high altitudes</u> have the problem of <u>inaccessibility</u> where roads are difficult to build and maintain in mountainous regions. This can make <u>access</u> to <u>natural resources</u> difficult and therefore makes the development of industry even harder.

- <u>Congestion</u>, <u>noise</u> and <u>pollution</u> are problems in LEDC cities too.

EXAMPLES

Peru has a high altitude, with many places that are hard to get to.

Mexico City and Nairobi in Kenya have problems with congestion, noise and pollution.

The Leisure Industry

People in MEDCs have increasing amounts of spare time which means that the leisure industry is growing quickly.

Leisure is a Growing Industry

Nowadays people have more <u>free time</u> — because the working week is shorter than it was 40 years ago and <u>new laws</u> give workers the right to a minimum number of days' holiday per year.

<u>Flexible working hours</u> mean people take their leisure at different times, while old attitudes that Sunday was a day of rest have changed.

Also, <u>wages in MEDCs have risen</u> at a higher rate than the cost of living — so people have <u>more money</u> to spend.

The leisure industry <u>caters</u> for people's need to relax and do things they enjoy, but also <u>creates new activities</u>, e.g. kite surfing.

Examples include the <u>leisure centres</u> and <u>fitness clubs</u> that have grown up in towns to provide for the growing market.

The definition of leisure is changing — many people now see education and shopping as leisure activities rather than necessary tasks.

Increased leisure time

Tourism — an Expanding Leisure Industry

People are taking <u>longer</u> and more <u>expensive</u> holidays:

- People have more <u>disposable income</u> nowadays.

- Most jobs give at least three weeks of <u>paid holiday time</u> per year — many as much as five weeks.

- Many people now have <u>more than one</u> holiday each year.

- Travel has become <u>cheaper</u>, particularly air travel.

- <u>Jet aircraft</u> have made all parts of the world easily accessible.

<u>Tourism</u> has become a huge industry all over the world. It provides a huge amount of the <u>money</u> countries need for things like schools, hospitals and roads.

Tourism	→	MONEY →	Schools
		MONEY →	Hospitals
		MONEY →	Roads

Tourism provides money for important services

People want to Try New Kinds of Holidays

People are <u>increasingly aware</u> of new holiday destinations and are keen to visit unusual places.

They have become <u>more adventurous</u> and have <u>higher expectations</u> — people whose parents spent a week in the rain in Blackpool, now might prefer two weeks in the Caribbean sun.

Better than Blackpool

There are now <u>specialist activity holidays</u>, like bird-watching or pony-trekking.

<u>LEDCs</u> want a share of the <u>huge profits</u> of this industry — they promote themselves as <u>holiday destinations</u> to fund <u>development</u>, and they have the benefit of being <u>much cheaper</u> than many MEDC destinations.

EXAMPLE

Many people now think of shopping as a leisure activity rather than a necessity. Huge shopping malls have been built to meet the increased demand for shopping. Examples include:

Place	Shopping Centre
Sheffield	Meadowhall
Manchester	Trafford Centre
Gateshead	Metro Centre
Birmingham	Bull Ring

EXAMPLES

LEDC holiday destinations
Goa
The Gambia
Kenya

Specialist holidays
Safari
Sailing
Skiing
Cruises

Tourism and LEDCs

Tourism is increasingly important for LEDC economies. It has become the main industry in some LEDCs, replacing more traditional activities like agriculture.

Tourism is one Route to _Development_

Tourism brings <u>foreign money</u> into the LEDC, along with <u>new investment</u> — big companies build hotels and airports to profit from the tourist trade.

There are <u>new jobs</u> for the people, and <u>local businesses</u> are <u>strengthened</u>.

There can be a <u>knock-on effect</u> — other industries start to move to the LEDC as the <u>infrastructure</u> develops and <u>labour costs</u> are still cheaper than in MEDCs.

Tourism has Several _Disadvantages_

Building basic infrastructure is <u>expensive</u>, especially road and sewage systems.

Many of the <u>profits</u> go <u>abroad</u> — flights are arranged and paid for abroad, and hotels are often owned by multinational companies.

Increased <u>wealth</u> is <u>restricted</u> to the local area. The rest of the country stays <u>poor</u>.

Mass tourism is not <u>sustainable</u> (it damages the <u>environment</u>) and in the end people will become fed up with the crowds, pollution, spoilt beaches and sewage and they'll find somewhere else to go.

Local <u>customs</u> and <u>culture</u> may be <u>exploited</u> or <u>disappear</u> (see next page).

Ecotourism Reduces the Effect of Tourists

<u>Ecotourism</u> is a recent idea — specialist holidays for small groups living in <u>reserve zones</u>, eating <u>local food</u> and using simple <u>local accommodation</u>, allowing them to get really close to nature. Unlike mass tourism, ecotourism aims to be <u>sustainable</u> — causing as little <u>impact</u> as possible.

- <u>Small group numbers</u> means they can enter <u>sensitive areas</u> that others can't.

- These holidays are more <u>expensive</u>, so the income for the LEDC is better.

- Groups are <u>conservation-minded</u> and follow <u>strict guidelines</u>.

- Local culture and customs are <u>respected</u>.

Game Parks are Wildlife Preservation Areas

Safaris are popular holiday destinations in LEDCs like Kenya, Tanzania and India.

The animals in game parks can be seen in their <u>natural state</u> — they are a big attraction for visitors.

People are also attracted to the scenery in game parks — lakes and waterfalls are popular recreational sites.

<u>Accommodation</u> is often in tents and traditional buildings rather than conventional hotels.

Lion in his natural environment

Example: Tourism in Peru

Most tourists visit Peru to explore the <u>Andes mountains</u> and discover the <u>Inca</u> settlements. Tourism brings <u>money</u> to the area, but must be <u>managed</u> carefully.

There are <u>guidelines</u> in place as to how the area can be used by tourists — in this way, it can be <u>protected</u> for future generations. Tourism in Peru has benefited the <u>locals</u>, as many have been able to get well-paid <u>jobs</u> in the tourist industry and tourists can buy their <u>handicrafts</u>. Tourism in Peru has also benefited the <u>country</u> as a whole because it has raised its <u>profile</u> and increased the amount of <u>money</u> being spent in the country.

Inca settlement

EXAMPLES

Tourism brings new jobs for local people in hotels, shops, restaurants and as tour guides.
Local farmers will also have an improved income by being able to supply food to hotels.

EXAMPLES

Game parks
Masai Mara game reserve, Kenya
Zambezi national park, Zimbabwe

Game park recreation
Safaris
Hot air balloon flights
Water sports on lakes, like lake Nakuru in Kenya

WORLD LOCATION

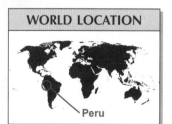

Peru

Tourism and Conflict

Pretty much everything people do causes <u>conflict</u> somewhere along the line — tourism is just the same. Learn why for your exams.

Tourism Depends on <u>Human</u> and <u>Natural Resources</u>

Art, culture, architecture and museums are <u>human resources</u>.

Climatic and physical features are <u>natural resources</u> — warm sunshine, snow, sandy beaches or mountains are good examples of valuable natural resources.

Tourist <u>Demands</u> Cause <u>Conflict</u> in MEDCs

Demand for <u>access</u> to tourist areas increases <u>road construction</u> and <u>building</u> of other facilities, often on farmland or open spaces.

<u>Job-providing industries</u> like quarrying can <u>ruin</u> a <u>landscape</u> that attracts tourists.

<u>Residents</u> in tourist areas like National Parks might want new <u>facilities</u> like supermarkets and shopping centres which visitors and planners may think are <u>not in keeping</u> with the area.

<u>Open land</u> is seen as <u>recreation space</u>, but it also provides <u>farmers' livelihoods</u>.

Some <u>recreational activities</u> are <u>incompatible</u> and can't happen together.

Conflict-causing events in MEDC tourist areas

Conflict in LEDCs comes from <u>Tourist Development</u>

LEDCs promote tourism in game parks, but <u>too many visitors</u> can ruin the wild animals' natural habitat so the animals are forced to move to a new area.

The demand for <u>food</u> by tourists can also cause conflict because sometimes farmers are forced to expand their farms into conservation areas and destroy <u>natural habitats</u>. Problems can be caused if animals from game parks damage local farmers' land.

Developments to accommodate tourists can also cause conflict because natural habitats are destroyed when facilities like <u>hotels</u> are built.

LEDC <u>Cultures</u> are often Challenged by Tourism

Tourists bring their <u>own culture</u> with them and often <u>don't respect</u> the culture they're visiting. <u>Attitudes</u> in an <u>LEDC</u> can be <u>challenged</u> by visitors from an <u>MEDC</u> — often MEDC women <u>dress</u> and <u>act</u> in a way that <u>offends</u> the people of the LEDC — especially in <u>Islamic countries</u> where it is usual for women to cover their skin in public places.

Local women cover up

<u>MEDC tourists</u> are seen as being <u>rich</u> — and some <u>LEDC people</u> have this as a <u>goal</u>. Lots of people in LEDCs <u>copy</u> foreign attitudes to try <u>to achieve</u> this goal. <u>Development</u> encourages <u>changing attitudes</u> — indigenous cultures <u>change</u> or <u>disappear</u> as locals adopt the practices of tourists from MEDCs.

Tourists can offend locals

For the exam you need to learn a case study about economic change in a country. You need to know the location of the country, the reasons for the economic change and the results of the changes.

Case Study: _Economic Change in Malaysia_

There has been a shift from primary to secondary industry:

Traditionally, the dominant industry in Malaysia has been primary industry. Agricultural activities like <u>rubber tapping</u> and <u>timber growing</u> were the main source of income.

Rubber tapping

WORLD LOCATION

Malaysia

However, in the last 40 years, there has been a significant increase in the <u>manufacturing</u> and <u>service industries</u> in Malaysia. Between 1960 and 1990 the percentage of employment in Malaysia in secondary and tertiary industry doubled. Investment by MNCs means that Malaysia is now a Newly Industrialised Country (NIC).

S.E. ASIAN LOCATION

Philippines
South China Sea
Malaysia
Indonesia

Malaysia has developed its manufacture of <u>high-value goods</u> such as cars — for example, in 1985, the government funded the <u>Proton</u> car company. In more recent years, Malaysia has moved on to concentrate on <u>research and development</u> in areas like electronics, IT and multimedia. There have also been a series of '<u>prestige</u>' projects — for example, there is a new capital city at Putrajaya planned for completion in 2008.

Malaysia is attractive to MNCs:

MNCs have been attracted to locate in Malaysia for a few different reasons:

- Malaysia is in a <u>good location</u> for MNCs because it provides good access to international markets like Japan, Taiwan, Singapore and China. Malaysia also has a good <u>home market</u> for manufactured products.

- Malaysia offers <u>cheap labour</u> for the manufacturing industry. It is much cheaper for MNCs to have their production in Malaysia than in MEDCs, where the cost of labour is higher and there are tighter working regulations.

- <u>Land</u> for industrial plants is <u>cheap</u>.

- The Malaysian government offer <u>low tax rates</u> as an incentive to encourage investment by MNCs.

EXAMPLE

This image of a city in Malaysia shows how it is no longer an LEDC.
The money from foreign investment has been used to develop an attractive CBD with high-class office facilities.

Economic change in Malaysia has both advantages and disadvantages:

Advantages	Disadvantages
More jobs are available in Malaysia. The new jobs are in secondary and tertiary industries and are better paid than jobs in farming.	Pollution has increased because of the new industries.
Some employers have provided training for their staff so more people have some education than in the past.	Some workers have been exploited by MNCs because Malaysia's employment regulations are not very strict.
The infrastructure in Malaysia has been vastly improved to accommodate the new businesses. There are now three-lane motorways, dual carriageways, new airports and a new deep port for sea freight.	The majority of the profits made by MNCs are exported from Malaysia to MEDCs where MNCs have their headquarters.
Malaysia is now an NIC.	If there is a global recession the MNCs might withdraw from Malaysia causing unemployment and economic decline.

Revision Summary

This section is all about how economies are changing. These changes include the obvious things like the decline of heavy industry in the UK as well as the things that don't come to mind as easily — like the need to develop sustainable tourism in Peru. For any question on changing economies the most important thing you need to know is <u>why</u> things are changing and what <u>effect</u> the changes have on industry, the environment and people's quality of life.

1) What are the two main causes of the decline of traditional manufacturing in MEDCs?

2) Which sector employs most people in the UK: primary, secondary or tertiary?

3) What is a footloose industry?

4) Give an example of a science park and explain what kind of businesses are located there.

5) What is the difference between formal and informal employment in LEDCs?

6) What does 'NIC' stand for?

7) What characteristics encouraged foreign investments in NICs?

8) Name the 'Tiger Economies'.

9) What does 'CAP' stand for?

10) Why have 25% of the UK hedgerows been removed since 1945?

11) Describe two problems that the introduction of milk quotas caused.

12) What is the 'set aside' policy? Why was it introduced?

13) Give three examples of farm diversification schemes.

14) Name two examples of ESAs.

15) Why did the Indian government establish the National Information Technology Task Force? What effects has it had?

16) Describe how market trends can cause economic growth and decline.

17) Give another name for multinational companies.

18) Name two examples of MNCs.

19) List five advantages and five disadvantages of MNCs for countries where they operate.

20) Name seven ways of reducing congestion.

21) How can the climate affect transport in LEDCs?

22) Write a paragraph to explain why the leisure industry is growing.

23) Why are LEDCs growing in popularity as holiday destinations?

24) What is a game park?

25) In what ways does ecotourism aim to be sustainable?

26) How can the demands of tourists cause conflict in MEDCs?

27) What effect can tourism have on culture in LEDCs?

28) What were the traditional industries in Malaysia?

29) Give four reasons why Malaysia is attractive to MNCs.

30) Write a mini-essay discussing the advantages and disadvantages of economic change in Malaysia.

EXAM TIP

There are quite a lot of complicated terms and abbreviations in this section. If you're finding it difficult to learn them all then try making a list of them all to use when you're revising.

Contrasts in Development

Developed and developing countries have different characteristics around the world.

The World's Wealth is Not Shared Out Equally

The world can be divided into richer and poorer countries — 25% of the world's population own 80% of the world's wealth.

Wealthier countries are known as More Economically Developed Countries (MEDCs), or developed countries.

MEDC city

Poorer countries are described as Less Economically Developed Countries, or LEDCs — they're also called Developing Countries or the Third World. This term came from a time when MEDCs were known as the 'First World', the former communist countries were the 'Second World', and the rest were the 'Third World'.

The term '<u>development</u>' refers to how mature a country's economy, infrastructure and social systems are — the more developed a country's economic systems are, the wealthier it is.

The 'development gap' is the contrast between rich and poor countries. It's best shown by comparing the estimated GNP per capita of a rich and a poor country. (The GNP per capita is the Gross National Product per capita — see next page.)

LEDC village

The North-South Divide Separates Developed and Developing Worlds

The map of rich and poor countries can be split by a line called the North-South Divide.

The richer countries are almost all in the Northern Hemisphere — except Australia and New Zealand. Poorer countries are mostly in the tropics and the Southern Hemisphere.

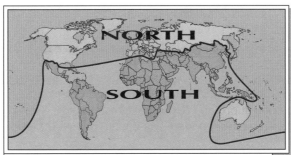
The North-South Divide, as defined in the Brandt Report (1979)

Places that suffer natural disasters like droughts are often Developing Countries.

The richer countries mainly have temperate (moderate) climates and good natural resources (although there are exceptions, like Japan). This meant these countries developed their industry first and became dominant in the world economy.

The explanations for the North-South Divide have as much to do with political history as they do with physical geography. Many MEDCs had colonies in LEDCs and there are still restrictions imposed on world trade — this means the development gap is getting wider.

Measuring Development

The concept of LEDCs and MEDCs is fairly straightforward, but measuring a country's development is more tricky — because there are so many indicators of development. (NB Indicators are also known as indices.)

Development Indices — Comparing Development Levels

The following indicators can be used to measure development:

1) Gross Domestic Product (GDP): Total value of goods and services produced in a year per total population. Gross National Product (GNP) is similar but includes invisible earnings like foreign investments. This is useful but says nothing about distribution of wealth — it can therefore be misleading. GNP or GDP per capita are therefore more useful — they reveal the total value of goods and services produced in a year per person.

2) Life expectancy: Average age a person can expect to live to — this is higher for women.

3) Infant mortality rate: Number of babies who die under 1 year old, per thousand live births.

4) Calorie intake: Average number of calories eaten per day — at least 2500 are needed for an adult to stay healthy.

5) Energy consumption: Weight of coal (or equivalent) used per person per year — an indication of levels of industry.

6) Urban population: Percentage of the total population living in towns and cities.

7) Literacy rates: Percentage of adults who can read well enough to get by.

	UK	ETHIOPIA
①	GNP per capita $28,700	GNP per capita $100
②	women 77 yrs men 74 yrs	women 48 yrs men 46 yrs
③	6 per thousand	120 per thousand
④	3,317 per day	1,610 per day
⑤	54 tonnes	0.03 tonnes
⑥	80%	15%
⑦	99%	36%
⑧	300	32,500

Comparison of development indices for the UK and Ethiop.

8) People per doctor: Number of potential patients for every doctor.

Many of these indices are linked, and relationships can be identified — for example countries with high GDP tend to have high urban populations and consume a lot of energy. These relationships can also be used to identify a country's level of development.

There are Two Main Problems with the Indices

Some countries may appear to be developed according to some indices but not others — as a country develops, some aspects develop before others. No measurement should be used on its own — it should be balanced with other indices to avoid any inaccuracies.

Up to date information isn't always available — maybe because a country doesn't have the administration necessary to compile and publish it, or because they don't want the information to be available publicly. This can make comparisons between countries difficult.

Investment in LEDCs

Manufacturing industry used to be mainly found in MEDCs, but this is changing.
Many multinational companies (MNCs) are now investing in LEDC locations.

Manufacturing Industry has _Changed Location_

Over recent years there has been a shift in the location of
manufacturing industry from MEDCs to LEDCs.

There are a variety of reasons for this shift:

- Cheap labour — A hardworking and efficient workforce is available at a
  cheap rate in LEDCs. This is one of the most important factors encouraging
  manufacturing industry to locate in LEDCs. Companies will be able to make
  a bigger profit if they are spending less on the wages of their workforce.

- Lax regulations — Companies often take advantage of lax regulations in
  LEDCs. Health and safety standards are often lower in LEDCs than in MEDCs,
  so companies can get away with spending less on safety. There may also be
  fewer regulations about pollution, so companies can save money through
  not having to use expensive pollution-reducing procedures.

- Market — Companies situated in LEDCs have access to expanding markets.
  This is particularly true in south east Asian countries, where many of the
  home markets have developed over recent years.

- Cheaper land — The site for the development of the company is often cheaper
  in LEDCs than it would be in MEDCs, letting companies save money on land.

> **EXAMPLES**
>
> **Pepsi has invested in
> factories in Brazil and other
> parts of South America.
> Nike and Reebok have also
> invested in factories in
> South America.
> Other companies, such as
> Sony and Samsung have
> located in South East Asia.**

There are _Advantages_ and _Disadvantages_ for LEDCs

There are direct advantages and disadvantages of investment for LEDCs
(see page 62), and also 'multiplier effects' — knock-on effects such as
education for workers' families.

Some countries can develop from LEDCs into NICs due to investment
and increase their wealth enough to escape many of the traps of LEDCs.
NICs like Malaysia have helped to increase LEDCs' share of world
manufacturing, and this share is predicted to continue to rise.

However, the results of investment aren't always so positive.
Companies usually invest in LEDCs for business reasons rather than
from a direct desire to improve the LEDC, and the type of industry
that's invested in affects how beneficial it is for the LEDC. For example:

> **EXAMPLES**
>
> **Countries which have
> done well out of
> investment and have
> become NICs include
> Taiwan, Korea, Brazil
> Mexico and Argentina
> (see page 58 for more
> information about NICs).**

- Investment in plantations like tea, coffee,
  cotton and palm oil, is less successful for
  LEDCs than more labour intensive
  manufacturing industries, like car assembly
  plants. Wages are generally lower for
  plantation work, and the employment is
  usually informal (e.g. seasonal or part-time).

Tea picker in a tea plantation

- Investment in capital-intensive industries
  like oil and chemicals mean that there aren't
  many jobs generated for the LEDC —
  machines do the work rather than people.

The Question of Aid

Aid is the giving of resources (goods or services) — usually from MEDCs to LEDCs, either in an emergency or to promote long-term development.

Aid can be _Bilateral_, _Multilateral_ or _Non-Governmental_

Bilateral aid is aid given directly from one government to another. It could be money, training, personnel, technology, food or other supplies. It could be tied aid, which means the donor country puts conditions on the aid,

We need tractors. Can you help?

We will give you the money, but you must buy them from us.

LEDC   MEDC

Tied aid

usually to benefit itself. An MEDC can seem to be giving aid, but really be getting its money back and helping its own industry.

Multilateral aid is aid, usually money, given through an agency such as the World Bank. The agency then distributes the aid to countries that need it.

Non-governmental aid is given through organisations like charities. This type of aid is very varied, and can include small scale development projects as well as emergency help during disasters.

There are Arguments _For and Against_ Giving Aid

In Favour of Giving Aid	Against Giving Aid
Emergency aid in times of disaster has saved lives and reduced people's misery.	Aid can increase the dependency of LEDCs on the donor country.
Development projects such as provision of clean water can lead to long-term improvements to living standards.	Inappropriate food aid can lead to a taste for imported food which the country can't afford and can't grow itself.
Assistance in developing natural resources and power supplies benefits the economy.	Profit from large projects can go to multinationals and donors, rather than the country that is supposed to be receiving the aid.
Aiding industrial development can create jobs and improve the infrastructure.	Aid doesn't always reach the people who need it and can be kept by corrupt officials.
Aid for agriculture can help to increase the food supply.	Aid can be spent on 'prestige projects' or in urban areas rather than in areas of real need.
Provision of medical training and equipment can improve health and standards of living.	Aid can be used as a weapon to exert political pressure on the receiving country.

The poorest countries don't always get most aid. Some MEDCs help LEDCs for political purposes rather than on the basis of need.

So aid can often create as many, or more, problems as it solves.

Development Projects

<u>Development projects</u> are schemes promoting development in LEDCs — often funded by aid money. They range from huge multi-million dollar schemes to small self-help projects.

Large Scale _Prestige Projects_ Don't Always _Succeed_

Some governments opt for <u>prestige projects</u> — expensive, well publicised schemes like dams providing water and electricity for large areas.

Prestige projects can be <u>successful</u>, but often they <u>fail</u> to achieve their aims. Some of the problems are outlined below.

EXAMPLES

Prestige projects
Aswan Dam, Egypt
Gezira irrigation scheme, Sudan

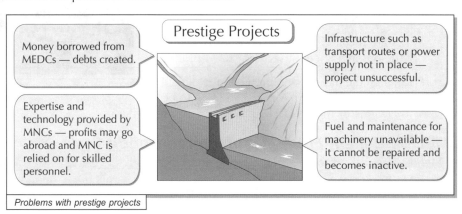

Prestige Projects

Money borrowed from MEDCs — debts created.

Infrastructure such as transport routes or power supply not in place — project unsuccessful.

Expertise and technology provided by MNCs — profits may go abroad and MNC is relied on for skilled personnel.

Fuel and maintenance for machinery unavailable — it cannot be repaired and becomes inactive.

Problems with prestige projects

Self-Help Schemes and _Small Scale Projects_ Can Lead to _Long-Term Development_

Small-scale projects are <u>government</u> or <u>charity funded</u>. They provide <u>specific improvements</u> for a small area and prioritise <u>training</u> for local people — which means they become <u>self-sufficient</u>, needing no outside help.

There are <u>three main categories</u> of small scale project:

- Provision of <u>basic necessities</u> to improve <u>standards of living</u>, such as clean water and sanitation, safe storage of agricultural produce or road building.

- Provision of <u>essential services</u> such as a health clinic or a school.

- Setting up co-operatives to facilitate <u>low cost borrowing</u> and <u>saving schemes</u> run by local people to allow investment in agriculture or employment.

Small scale projects

Small Scale Projects Have Several _Advantages_:

- <u>Costs</u> are <u>lower</u> and do not incur large debts.

- <u>Training</u> has long-term benefits for local people.

- Local people have <u>ownership</u> and don't have to rely on outsiders.

- <u>Appropriate technology</u> is used and maintenance is less of a problem.

KEY TERM

**Appropriate technology:
Development schemes
which are right for the
people and the place.
The technology and
processes used in the
project have to be
affordable and sustainable.**

International Trade

Trade is the exchange of goods and services between countries.
World trade patterns are an important aspect of development —
they seriously influence a country's economy.

World Trade Patterns Benefit MEDCs more than LEDCs

LEDCs have a relatively small share of world trade (except NICs),
and rely heavily on primary products for export income.

Primary products have four disadvantages for LEDCs:

* Raw materials have a lower value
  than manufactured goods.

* Prices are dictated by the MEDC buyers,
  not the producing countries.

* Prices fluctuate yearly and prediction is difficult.

LEDCs rely on primary products

* Man-made alternatives to some raw materials reduce demand.

> **EXAMPLES**
>
> **Effects of man-made alternatives on raw materials:**
> * **The use of polyester for clothing has reduced the demand for cotton.**
> * **Plastics reduce demand for rubber.**

MEDCs Benefit From Manufactured Goods

Manufactured goods have a higher value and hold steady prices,
as the graph below shows.

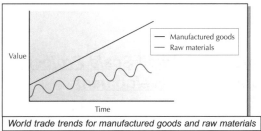

World trade trends for manufactured goods and raw materials

There are two important points:

* The price of manufactured goods is rising faster so the gap between the
  prices of manufactured goods and raw materials is widening — rich
  countries are getting richer and poor countries are getting relatively poorer.

* Prices of manufactured goods are steady, while prices of raw materials
  often fluctuate. This makes it difficult for LEDCs to predict their earnings.

Trade Blocs are Countries who are Trading Partners

Trade blocs are groups of countries with similar characteristics who have
trade agreements benefiting the member countries.

An important feature of trade blocs is that member states don't charge tariffs on
trade with each other, to encourage trade within the group — tariffs are taxes
levied on imports to make them more expensive than domestically produced
goods. They are higher for manufactured goods than for raw materials —
affecting LEDCs in many ways:

* LEDCs can't compete — income from raw materials is low, and heavy
  tariffs are put on manufactured goods they produce for export to MEDCs.

* MEDCs can't lose — they import raw materials at low cost and put
  heavy tariffs on any manufactured goods from LEDCs, while trading
  freely between themselves.

So the current international trade system is not effective in narrowing the gap
between LEDCs and MEDCs. In fact, it is making the problem worse.

> **EXAMPLES**
>
> | Trade Blocs |
> | --- |
> | EU (European Union) |
> | OPEC (Organisation of Petroleum Exporting Countries) |
> | NAFTA (North American Free Trade Association) |

Case Study

In this section you need to know one case study on aid. You have to learn who received the aid, why it was needed, and what type of aid it was.

Case Study: _Aid to Ethiopia_

Ethiopia needed relief aid in the 1980s

Ethiopia suffered a famine in the 1980s, reaching its peak in 1984. The rains had been below average for a few years, causing drought conditions. The majority of Ethiopians are subsistence farmers, so when the drought caused crops to fail, there was little food for individuals to fall back on. People living near the borders in the north and south were the worst affected — approximately 500 000 people died in 1984.

The Ethiopian government couldn't provide food aid for the people who needed it, because the country was involved in a civil war. They'd already spent a third of their budget on the armed forces.

Relief aid took a while to happen

The Ethiopian government covered up news of the famine, so it took a while for the world to even find out. When they did find out, other governments were reluctant to provide aid, because the Ethiopian government was spending so much money on the civil war and weapons. It was only due to pressure from aid agencies that aid was provided, but this wasn't enough to make a big difference.

In the end, the UK Disasters Emergency Fund, which is made up of charities such as Oxfam and Cafod, raised nearly £15 million. This was mostly used to provide food aid. The Ethiopian government gave some of this food aid to its armed forces, but most reached the people in need.

A big difference was made by the Irish pop star Bob Geldof. He organised 'Band Aid', where nearly 40 of the UK and Ireland's best-known singers recorded a song called 'Do they know it's Christmas?'.

This raised approximately £8 million worldwide. He also organised a 16 hour concert called 'Live Aid' which consisted of massive numbers of famous names. Overall, about £110 million was raised. So Ethiopia did eventually receive a lot of short-term aid.

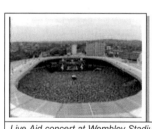
Live Aid concert at Wembley Stadium

Ethiopia still needs aid

Ethiopia has now overthrown its military government, so it has a chance to start again. However, half the population still lives in poverty and some areas still have severe food shortages. If the rains fail, people are still at risk of famine and still have to rely on food aid.

The charity Cafod is now providing Ethiopia with long-term aid, helping to develop agriculture so that farmers can eventually meet their own needs and survive through drought. This includes providing drought-resistant seeds and trees, digging wells, marketing excess produce and providing loans for tools.

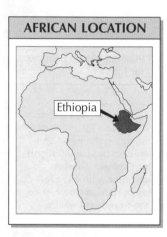

WORLD LOCATION

Ethiopia

AFRICAN LOCATION

Ethiopia

Revision Summary

This section is all about the difference between MEDCs and LEDCs. It's also about what can be done to try and lessen this difference. Unfortunately, a lot things are actually making the difference worse. This is a very tricky subject, but a really important one, so give it a lot of attention. Have a go at these questions and keep going over them until you can answer them all.

1) What exactly does the term 'development' refer to?

2) What is the development gap? What is the best way of showing it?

3) Draw a rough sketch of the world to show the North-South Divide.

4) How do LEDCs and MEDCs differ in terms of climate, resources and industry?

5) Why is GNP per capita a better indicator of development than just GNP?

6) Name five other development indices.

7) Compare two named countries using the development indices.

8) What are the two main problems with using development indices?

9) Give three reasons why TNCs have invested in factories in LEDCs.

10) Write a mini-essay discussing whether investment by TNCs benefits LEDCs.

11) Explain how two different types of aid work.

12) Why is tied aid not actually very charitable?

13) Write a mini-essay to discuss the arguments for and against giving aid.

14) Give an example of aid given in return for a political advantage.

15) What are prestige projects?

16) Name two problems associated with prestige projects.

17) Give two examples of small scale self-help projects.
How do they help lead to long-term development?

18) What is appropriate technology?

19) Sketch a graph of the world trade trends for manufactured goods and raw materials.

20) How do the trends shown in the graph affect the development gap?

21) What are trade blocs?

22) Do trade blocs benefit LEDCs? Explain your answer.

23) Why didn't the Ethiopian government have enough money for food aid in the 1980s?

24) What are Live Aid and Band Aid?

25) Is Ethiopia still at risk of famine?

26) List some types of long-term aid that could help Ethiopia.

EXAM TIP

There are always lots of debates over trade agreements and aid, so it's a good idea to keep watching the news and reading the paper. If you can answer an exam question with a really up-to-date example, then the examiners will be very impressed.

Population Distribution

Population distribution is where people live — this can be on a global, regional or local scale.

Population Distribution — *Where People Live*

Places with lots of people usually have habitable environments. They are either:

- wealthy and industrial e.g. Europe, Japan, eastern USA.

- poor with rapidly growing populations e.g. India, Kenya.

Places with few people are usually hostile environments.

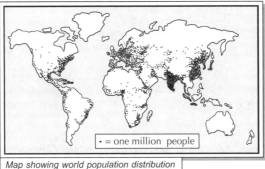

• = one million people

Map showing world population distribution

Large Populations Live in *Accessible Areas* with *Good Resources*

River valleys are sheltered. The river provides a transport and communication link as well as a water supply.

Lowland plains are flat with fertile soils allowing productive farming and easy communication.

Areas rich in natural resources can be important sources of materials for industry. Resources include fossil fuels (coal, oil and gas) and ores like iron and bauxite.

Coastal plains often have moderate climates and good access for international trade because they have sea ports.

EXAMPLES	
Areas of high population	
River Valleys	Ganges Valley (India), Rhine Valley (Germany)
Fertile lowland plains	East Anglia (cereals), Denmark (dairy farming)
Natural resources (coal)	South Wales coalfield, Ruhr Valley (Germany)
Coastal plains	New York

Few People Live in Places *Without Resources*

Areas with extreme climates are almost empty. This is not only extremes of temperature — lack of precipitation (aridity) is just as important. Humans can cope with pretty hot and cold temperatures but we can't cope without water. Even so, very hot and cold places such as Antarctica and the Sahara Desert are good examples of places too extreme for people to live in.

High altitudes are inaccessible, have poor soils and steep slopes which means that farming is difficult. This combination means that this environment can support few people. A good example is the Andes mountains in South America.

EXAMPLES	
Areas of low population	
Extreme climates	Antarctica, Sahara (N Africa)
High altitudes	Andes (S America), Himalayas (Asia), Atlas Mts (Morocco)

Accessibility of areas for population

Population Growth

Population growth is a worrying matter. In some countries, the population is fairly stable, but in others, it's growing so <u>fast</u> that there's a strain on resources.

Population Growth is Affected by <u>Three</u> Factors

<u>Birth rate</u> — number of live babies born per thousand of the population per year.

<u>Death rate</u> — number of deaths per thousand of the population per year.

<u>Migration</u> — number of people moving in or out.
(<u>Immigration</u> is people moving into an area, <u>emigration</u> is people moving away.)

Factors which lead to <u>high death rates</u> include a lack of <u>health care</u>, poor <u>diet</u>, lack of clean <u>water</u>, poor <u>sanitation</u> and <u>war</u>.
For death rates to fall, these factors need to improve.

SUMMARY

Factors leading to population growth:

- **high birth rate**
- **low death rate**
- **high immigration**
- **low emigration**

The World's Population is <u>Growing</u> Very Rapidly

The graph shows <u>world population growth</u>. It is not just the increase that is important — the <u>rate of increase</u> is getting faster.

The 20th century has seen a <u>population explosion</u>.
This means that a dramatic <u>drop</u> in the <u>death rate</u> has led to very rapid population growth.

The difference between the birth and death rates is the <u>natural increase</u> or <u>natural decrease</u>. (It's '<u>increase</u>' if the birth rate is higher and '<u>decrease</u>' if the death rate is higher.)

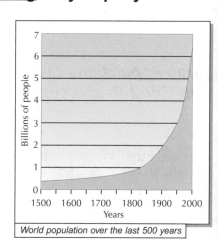

World population over the last 500 years

EXAM TIP

Overpopulation is a much more established and widespread problem than underpopulation. China has been trying to cope with its massive population for years. Underpopulation is rare — Switzerland and Germany now have very low birth rates and are starting to show signs of it.

The <u>Demographic Transition Model</u> Describes Population Growth

The population of a country changes over four stages of the demographic transition model. <u>Stage five</u> has been added to show the recent <u>population decline</u> in some <u>MEDCs</u>.

EXAMPLES

Stages of the demographic transition model:

Stage 1	Rainforest tribes in South America
Stage 2	Sri Lanka
Stage 3	China
Stage 4	Japan, UK
Stage 5	Germany

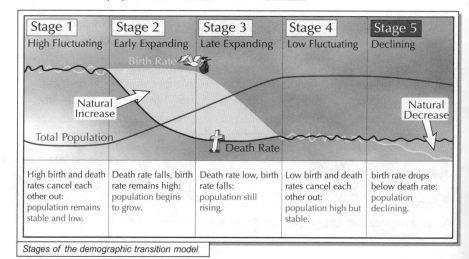

Stage 1	Stage 2	Stage 3	Stage 4	Stage 5
High Fluctuating	Early Expanding	Late Expanding	Low Fluctuating	Declining
High birth and death rates cancel each other out: population remains stable and low.	Death rate falls, birth rate remains high: population begins to grow.	Death rate low, birth rate falls: population still rising.	Low birth and death rates cancel each other out: population high but stable.	birth rate drops below death rate: population declining.

Stages of the demographic transition model

Population Structure

Population structure is the number of males and females in different age groups.
It's often shown as a <u>pyramid</u> with males and females on each side and the
different ages making up the different sized <u>layers</u>.

Population Pyramids Show Population Structure

There are two basic population pyramid shapes.

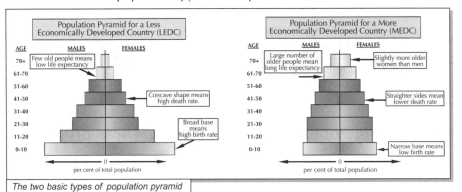

The two basic types of population pyramid

There are <u>3 common variations</u> on these basic shapes.

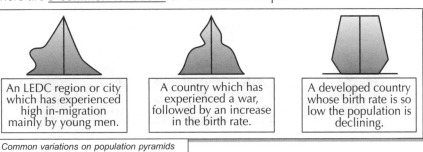

| An LEDC region or city which has experienced high in-migration mainly by young men. | A country which has experienced a war, followed by an increase in the birth rate. | A developed country whose birth rate is so low the population is declining. |

Common variations on population pyramids

Demographic Terms are Used to Describe Populations

A high <u>birth rate</u> or <u>death rate</u>, or a rising population indicates an <u>LEDC</u>
(i.e. <u>stage 1, 2 or 3</u> of the demographic transition model — see page 78).
More children are born in LEDCs because less <u>birth control</u> is used.
This is due to cultural and religious pressure, lack of contraception or
lack of birth control education.

<u>Infant mortality rate</u> — number of babies per thousand live births dying
before they are a year old. A high infant mortality rate indicates an <u>LEDC</u>.
This is because health care is worse in LEDCs.

<u>Life expectancy</u> — the average number of years a person can expect to live.
A high life expectancy indicates a good health care system and an <u>MEDC</u>.

<u>Economically active</u> — people between 16 and 64 years old
(capable of earning a living). A high proportion of economically
active people indicates high earning power — an MEDC.

<u>Dependants</u> — people of non-working age supported by the
economically active. A high number of young dependants indicates
a high birth rate and an LEDC. A high number of elderly dependants
indicates a long life expectancy and an MEDC.

Population Dependency in LEDCs & MEDCs

Population dependency is a ratio comparing the amount of people of <u>working age</u> (16 to 64) with the number of <u>dependants</u> — people aged under 16 or over 65.

Dependency is Measured Using the <u>Dependency Ratio</u>

It's normally written as a single number which is the number of dependants for every <u>one hundred</u> people of working age.
The dependency ratio is worked out using this formula:

$$\frac{\text{number of children (0-15) and old people (65+)}}{\text{number of people of working age (16–64)}} \times 100$$

<u>High Dependency Levels</u> can Cause Serious Problems

<u>MEDCs</u> usually have a dependency ratio of 50 to 70.
<u>LEDCs</u> can have one of over 100.

The higher the dependency ratio, the more stretched the country becomes, as wealth has to be more <u>thinly spread</u>. This puts added pressure on the country's <u>workforce</u>. This is a particular problem in LEDCs, where there is less wealth to go round in the first place.

The problems of a high dependency ratio

<u>Young</u> Dependants Put a Strain on <u>LEDCs</u>

High levels of <u>education</u> provision and <u>health care</u> are needed for children and babies. Most LEDCs cannot afford this. A <u>population explosion</u> is <u>inevitable</u> as these young people reach child-bearing age.

The rapidly growing population need <u>housing</u>, and will need <u>employment</u> when they grow up. This is a serious concern for LEDCs.

<u>Elderly</u> Dependants Put a Strain on <u>MEDCs</u>

High levels of <u>health care</u> are needed — and long term care of the elderly can be expensive. Facilities such as <u>public transport</u> and <u>sheltered housing</u> are required and must be planned for.

Unlike young dependants, elderly dependants are <u>never</u> going to enter the workforce, therefore they are an <u>increasing</u> and <u>permanent financial strain</u> on the shrinking number of economically active members of the population.

Populations can be <u>stable</u> or even <u>declining</u>.
This can be serious for the country's future.

Migration

Migration is the movement of people from one area or country to another.

There are *Three Types* of *Migration*

International migration — when people move from one country to another. This can be across the world, or just a few miles over a border.

Regional migration — moving to another region in the same country.

Local migration — when people move a short distance within the same region.

Migration can be Classified by *Reason*

Migration happens because of push and pull factors:

- Push factors are the things about the origin that make someone decide to move. They are usually negative things such as lack of job or education opportunities.

- Pull factors are things about the destination that attract people. They are usually positive things such as job opportunities or the perception of a better standard of living.

> **EXAM TIP**
>
> Remember — it's usually a combination of push and pull factors that causes migration.

Be *Clear* about the *Right Terms*

The words used to describe migration all sound pretty similar, so learn them well.

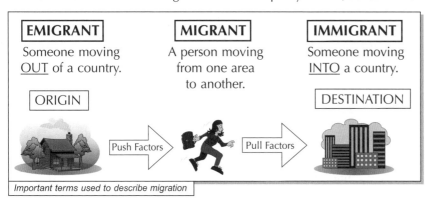

Important terms used to describe migration

Common Migration Types and their *Push and Pull Factors*

International migration from LEDCs to MEDCs is usually economic migrants searching for a higher standard of living.

Some international migration is from MEDC to MEDC due to job opportunities or warmer climates. A 'brain drain' is when highly qualified people move abroad to better opportunities.

Rural-urban migration is movement from the countryside to the cities, common in LEDCs where facilities and opportunities are better in urban areas.

Counter-urbanisation in MEDCs is movement out of cities into rural areas due to a perception of a more relaxed lifestyle, and lower pollution levels. Commuting (living in one place and working in another) has increased this trend.

Refugees are people who've been forced to leave their country due to war, hardship, natural disasters or political oppression. These can be large numbers or individuals.

EXAMPLES	
Types of migration	
Economic migrants	Mexico to USA
Climate	UK to Australia
Brain Drain	Scientists moving from UK to USA (better paid)
Rural-urban	Mexican villages to Mexico City
Counter-urbanisation	Inner London to Kent
Refugees	Kosovans moving from Albania to UK in 1999 due to war

Managing Population Growth

Population growth needs to be <u>controlled</u>, because the bigger the population, the greater the demand on <u>resources</u>.

Increasing the <u>Food Supply</u> can Cause Problems

There are many methods of increasing food supply to feed an exploding population, but they all have drawbacks.

<u>Irrigation of arid land</u> can increase the farming area. Schemes can be high-tech and expensive or simple and inexpensive, but can leave the soil salty.

<u>Marshland can be drained</u> to increase the farming land. This is usually expensive and is mostly done in MEDCs, but these areas can be prone to flooding.

<u>Fertilisers</u> can improve poor quality soil, but can be expensive and can cause <u>pollution</u> — for example by allowing excessive nitrate levels into the water supply.

<u>Pesticides</u> can increase crop yield. But they can be expensive, and can kill insects and animals — affecting the whole <u>food chain</u>.

<u>Pressure on the environment</u> comes as more people try to produce food from the same area of land. The results can be soil erosion, desertification and deforestation.

Sustainable Development can Slow Population Increase

To avoid causing long-term damage to the planet, the population increase has to be slowed.

LEDCs want to <u>reduce</u> the birth rate to slow population growth. To do this they need to break the <u>vicious circle</u> that causes the high birth rate.

The birth rate is influenced by <u>cultural</u> and <u>religious customs</u> which are very difficult to change. Many governments in LEDCs have encouraged <u>family planning</u> by educating women, opening clinics, and providing contraception.

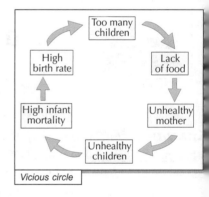

Vicious circle

Some countries have introduced <u>policies</u> aiming to increase the standard of living by reducing levels of malnutrition. This is linked with health policies.

For more about sustainable development, see pages 99-100.

Governments Play a Role in Controlling Population

Governments can either <u>encourage</u> or <u>refuse</u> immigration into their country.

On a local scale, <u>planning</u> and <u>employment</u> policies will affect decisions to move. For example, <u>government grants</u> are often given to companies to locate in <u>deprived areas</u>. This encourages people to move to the area for <u>jobs</u>, increasing the population and <u>improving</u> the area's economy and status.

Case Studies

You need to know case studies on population for your exam.
Two big issues are migration and population management,
so here are two case studies on them for you to learn:

Case Study 1: Rural to Urban Migration in <u>Mexico</u>

Many people in Mexico move from the countryside to towns and
cities such as Mexico City.

Push factors (away from the villages)	Pull factors (towards the towns and cities)
Lack of job opportunities. Agriculture is often the only choice.	Higher standard of living.
Pressure on the land — land is sub-divided within families, leaving small plots.	Bigger range of employment opportunities.
Increase in mechanisation reduces the amount of farm labour needed.	Better education — larger number of schools and better facilities.
Lack of services, e.g. hospitals, schools.	Better housing.
Lack of investment in rural areas.	Attraction of a busy, lively, modern city.

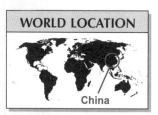

WORLD LOCATION

Mexico

Effects of migration

Cities like Mexico City suffer severe <u>overcrowding</u>. There is added pressure
on services such as hospitals and schools. However, the introduction of
people from different places has created a <u>social</u> and <u>ethnic mix</u> which makes
the city more 'vibrant'.

In the Mexican villages, there is often a loss of <u>community spirit</u>, as people move
away from the area. Rural areas are often left with an <u>elderly population</u> as
younger people move to the cities. However, there is less pressure on the land —
which increases <u>agricultural opportunities</u> for those that remain in the area.

AMERICAN LOCATION

USA
Mexico   Gulf of Mexico
Mexico City
Pacific Ocean   Central America

Case Study 2: Population Management in <u>China</u>

25% of the world's population is Chinese. In 1979, the Chinese government
introduced a '<u>One Child Policy</u>' to try and control population growth.

The policy

Couples had to gain <u>permission</u> from family planning officials for each birth.
<u>Birth control</u> was strictly enforced. People who had unauthorised children
were given big <u>fines</u>. Authorised children were given <u>benefits</u> such as free
education, health care, pensions and family benefits — unauthorised children
were given no benefits, schooling or employment opportunities.

In 1982, couples with more than two children were forced to be <u>sterilised</u> (mainly
women). Unauthorised pregnancies were often terminated by forced <u>abortion</u>.

WORLD LOCATION

China

Effects of the policy

The policy resulted in a high rate of <u>infanticide</u> (killing newborn children).
90% of foetuses aborted in China are <u>female</u> because Chinese tradition
values boys above girls.

Recently the government has used <u>less extreme</u> methods (e.g. birth
control education) with good results. It is estimated that without
the policy there would be an extra <u>320 million</u> people in China.

ASIAN LOCATION

Mongolia
Beijing
China
India

Revision Summary

Here we go again — lots more questions to test your knowledge. If you struggle with any of them, you need to go back through the section and keep going until you know it all — that way you'll have bags of confidence going into the exam.

1) Which parts of the world have very few people? Give some examples.

2) Which parts of the world have lots of people?
   Explain why and give some examples.

3) Define the following terms: birth rate, death rate, migration.

4) Sketch a graph of the world's population over the last 500 years.

5) What is a 'population explosion'? What causes it?

6) Explain what 'natural increase' and 'natural decrease' mean.

7) Draw the demographic transition model diagram.
   Name one country for each of the stages 2, 3, 4 and 5.

8) Draw and label the population pyramids for an LEDC and an MEDC.

9) Make a list of the population characteristics that can be identified in a population pyramid.

10) Draw and label a population pyramid shape for each of the following:
    a) An LEDC city or region which has experienced high in-migration especially by young men.
    b) A country that has experienced war followed by an increase in the birth rate.
    c) An MEDC with a birth rate so low the population is declining.

11) Define the term 'infant mortality rate'.

12) Do the following terms describe an LEDC or an MEDC?
    a) high life expectancy
    b) high number of elderly dependants
    c) high number of young dependants
    d) high infant mortality rate

13) Write down the formula for the dependency ratio.

14) Give three problems associated with a high number of young dependants.

15) Give three problems associated with an increasingly ageing population.

16) Name three types of migration.

17) What is counter-urbanisation?
    Give three reasons why it has become common in MEDCs.

18) Define these terms: immigrant, migrant, emigrant, refugee, brain drain.

19) Explain four ways in which food supply can be increased.

20) Name three environmental problems that are caused by trying to increase the food supply.

21) Why is it difficult to impose a population policy?

22) Describe the push and pull factors in rural to urban migration in Mexico.

23) What effects of rural to urban migration are found in Mexico?

24) How has China tried to manage its population growth?

Settlement Site and Situation

Site is the physical landscape a settlement is built on. Situation is the settlement location relative to the surrounding human environment (e.g. other settlements and roads). Settlements with good sites and situations often grow into large trading centres.

Site Factors Led to Different Types of Settlement

- Wet point sites: Water supply is a key factor — many settlements grew up near a river or spring. Spring line settlements are often found at the base of chalk scarps where the porous rock meets an impervious rock (which water can't soak into), such as clay, and springs are found.

- Dry point sites are found on areas of high land away from marshy areas or areas prone to flooding.

- Defensive sites originated on higher land which gave a good view of the surrounding area in case of attack. They are also sometimes found in the meanders of rivers where the river forms a natural barrier.

- Building materials were needed, originally wood or stone, so villages grew up where these were available. Wood was also important as fuel.

- Good farming land was essential to produce food — so many villages grew up in fertile lowlands.

- Accessibility and communication were essential — villages grew up at bridging points, crossroads and gaps between hills.

Wet point site

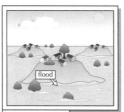
Dry point site

Defensive site

EXAMPLES	
Wet point sites	Edge of Salisbury plain and South Downs
Dry point site	Ely in Cambridgeshire
Defensive sites	Corfe Castle in Dorset
Building material site	Forest of Dean
Farming site	Vale of Evesham
Accessibility site	Fordingbridge in Hampshire

These site factors are no longer as important as they used to be. We can get round any of them if we want to with the aid of modern technology. For example, Las Vegas is built in an inhospitable desert — everything is transported in, from water to golf balls.

Settlements can be Dispersed or Nucleated

Nucleated settlements occur where a village is clustered around a central point or where it has a linear shape, following a road or river. They developed either where defence was important, around a water supply, or where co-operative farming took place.

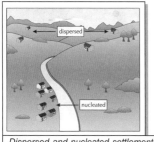
Dispersed and nucleated settlements

Dispersed settlements are those where the individual buildings are spread out. They developed where population is sparse and are common in areas of hill farming where farms cover large areas. The term dispersed is also commonly applied to the spread of settlements across a landscape as well as the shape of individual settlements.

FACT
Clues to the site factors of settlements are often found in their names: • **Oxford developed at a point where oxen could cross (ford) the river.** • **Cambridge developed where there was a bridge over the River Cam.**

The Settlement Hierarchy

A <u>settlement</u> is a place where people live. A <u>hierarchy</u> is a system of things that are ranked one above the other. So the <u>settlement hierarchy</u> is a rank order of settlements — easy.

Settlements are Ranked by <u>Population Size</u>

As settlement size <u>increases</u>, the number of settlements <u>decreases</u> — so there are many villages, but few conurbations.

The diagram below shows a pattern which is <u>generally</u> true, but be <u>careful</u> — there are examples of cities which are smaller than towns.

The <u>number of services</u> provided in a settlement <u>increases</u> with settlement size. Large places provide high and low order goods and services, small ones provide only low order goods and services.

EXAMPLES	
Conurbation	Birmingham
City	Lincoln
Large town	Doncaster, South Yorkshire
Small town	Gainsborough, Lincolnshire
Village	Heapham, Lincolnshire

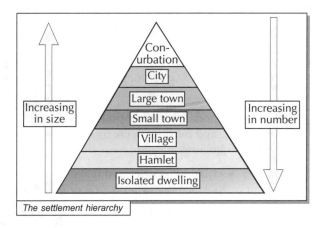

The settlement hierarchy

A Settlement's Size indicates its <u>Sphere of Influence</u>

KEY TERMS

**Low order goods —
everyday things like
bread, milk and
newspapers.**

**High order goods —
expensive or specialist
things like TVs, cars and
fishing tackle.**

The terms <u>sphere of influence</u>, <u>urban field</u>, <u>catchment area</u>, <u>market area</u> and <u>hinterland</u> all mean the same thing. It is the <u>area served</u> by the goods, services, administration and employment provided by a settlement (or 'central place') and which provides <u>agricultural produce</u> and <u>leisure facilities</u> (such as country parks, golf courses etc.) for the settlement.

<u>Small</u> central places have <u>small</u> hinterlands because the goods and services they provide are low order. <u>Large</u> central places have <u>large</u> hinterlands because they provide a wide variety of high order goods and services as well as low order goods and services, and people will travel further to use them.

The city serves the nearby towns...

...which in turn serve the nearby villages.

A city's hinterland

The Function of Settlements

Settlements have many functions but there is usually one principal function that characterises it the most. This function can change over time.

Settlements can be Classified by _Function_

A settlement's function is its main <u>economic activity</u> — most cities have <u>more</u> than one:

- A <u>retail function</u> — when a settlement is the <u>main shopping centre</u> in the area. These settlements are <u>easily accessible</u> as they have to attract people from the surrounding area. Your local large shopping centre is a good example.

A town might have a retail function...

- An <u>industrial</u> town or city — where <u>manufacturing</u> is the <u>main employer</u>. Many industrial towns are associated with a <u>particular industry</u>, and often it's because of the availability of <u>natural resources</u> in the local area.

...or an industrial function...

EXAMPLES
During the Industrial Revolution, the fast flowing streams of the Pennines and the availability of coal and iron ore led to the growth of cities like Manchester (cotton industry), Leeds (woollen industry) and Sheffield (steel industry).

...or function as a resort

- <u>Ports</u> are vital to <u>international trade</u>, and the UK's ports became important places in the eighteenth and nineteenth centuries. Some ports are still major cities because of this history.
- <u>Cultural centres</u> and <u>university towns</u> have a reputation for a cultural or educational service.
- <u>Resorts</u> are <u>holiday centres</u>, usually on the coast. They often have their own distinct characteristics. Resorts need facilities and services to cope with high numbers of <u>temporary residents</u> and the <u>permanent resident population</u> may be small.
- <u>Administrative centres</u> such as county towns employ a high number of civil servants and are the <u>centres of local government</u>.

EXAMPLES	
Industrial towns	Manchester, Leeds, Sheffield
Ports	Bristol, Liverpool
Cultural centres/ university towns	Bath, Oxford
Resorts	Blackpool, Bournemouth, Margate

Settlement Function can _Change_ over Time

Settlements change for individual reasons, but the causes can be summarised into <u>three categories</u>:

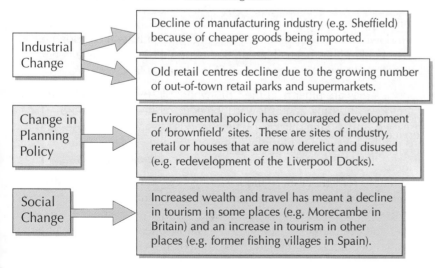

Industrial Change
→ Decline of manufacturing industry (e.g. Sheffield) because of cheaper goods being imported.
→ Old retail centres decline due to the growing number of out-of-town retail parks and supermarkets.

Change in Planning Policy
→ Environmental policy has encouraged development of 'brownfield' sites. These are sites of industry, retail or houses that are now derelict and disused (e.g. redevelopment of the Liverpool Docks).

Social Change
→ Increased wealth and travel has meant a decline in tourism in some places (e.g. Morecambe in Britain) and an increase in tourism in other places (e.g. former fishing villages in Spain).

EXAMPLE
Dudley in the West Midlands is an example of a declining retail centre — it can't compete with the new Merry Hill retail park.

Urban Land Use in MEDCs

Land use is exactly what you'd expect it to be —
what land is <u>used for</u>, like for housing or factories.

Land Use Models Describe Patterns in Cities

Two models of land use that apply to MEDCs are the <u>concentric zone model</u>
(devised by Burgess) and the <u>sector model</u> (devised by Hoyt).

EXAM TIP

**These models are
generalisations, to give
you an idea of how
land use is roughly
organised. It doesn't
mean that all cities will
follow the same pattern,
and you shouldn't
expect them to. All cities
have their own little
quirks and differences.**

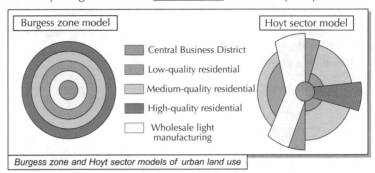

Burgess zone model		Hoyt sector model

Central Business District
Low-quality residential
Medium-quality residential
High-quality residential
Wholesale light manufacturing

Burgess zone and Hoyt sector models of urban land use

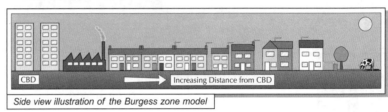

CBD → Increasing Distance from CBD

Side view illustration of the Burgess zone model

The <u>concentric zone model</u>, or Burgess zone model, says that the centre is the
oldest part of the city and building spreads out from the middle. This means the
<u>newest</u> parts of the city will be on the <u>edge</u> — the outer suburbs.

The <u>Hoyt sector model</u> expands this idea to take into account industrial
development along the main routeways into and out of a city.

MEDC Models have <u>Functional Zones</u> showing <u>Land Use</u>

The <u>Central Business District</u> (<u>CBD</u>) is the <u>commercial centre</u> of the city.
It contains shops and offices, transport routes meet here and it has high land
values as there is intense competition for space. Buildings are usually tall
and building density is very high. Very few people live in the CBD.

EXAM TIP

**See page 94 for more
about people living in
the country and
working in the city.
Also see page 95 for
more on the outer
edges of a city.**

The <u>zone of transition</u> or <u>inner city</u> is the area of <u>wholesale manufacturing</u>.
It is a mix of poorer quality housing and old industrial buildings which are
often run down, as well as newer housing and light industrial development
where derelict land has been cleared. Sometimes these areas have been
redeveloped and they can become desirable places to live.

The <u>housing areas</u> are <u>older near the CBD</u> where old terraced housing remains.
There are newer housing estates toward the edge of the city and more
expensive housing on the outskirts, where land is <u>cheaper</u> and houses and
gardens can be <u>bigger</u>. <u>Dormitory villages</u> on the edge of cities house
people who like to <u>live</u> in the country and <u>work</u> in the city.

It's important to remember these models are <u>generalisations</u> and real places are
all different. In recent years, out-of-town <u>shopping centres</u> and the replacement
of <u>inner city tower blocks</u> with housing estates on the <u>urban fringe</u> have begun
to <u>change</u> land use patterns. New housing is now often built on <u>brownfield
sites</u> (cleared derelict land) instead of the settlement's edges.

Urban Problems in MEDCs

Urban areas in MEDCs are gradually changing with time.

Traffic Problems are Common in MEDC Cities

The increase in <u>car ownership</u> and <u>commuting</u> means many <u>MEDC</u> cities have major <u>congestion</u> problems, particularly at rush hours. Some companies now allow <u>flexi-time</u> to help solve this problem, and cities have <u>traffic control</u> schemes such as 'park-and-ride' to try to ease congestion in the town centre.

<u>Time is money</u> to industry, so industry now tends to locate on the edge of cities near main roads to cut down time spent in traffic jams. This is one reason why many inner city industrial areas have become derelict.

<u>Pollution</u> caused by traffic fumes is a major problem in many <u>MEDC</u> cities. In the UK, the government is trying to tackle this with emissions limits on car exhausts.

Congestion, noise and pollution in cities

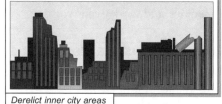

Derelict inner city areas

Manufacturing Decline has led to Inner City Problems

As <u>traditional manufacturing</u> near city centres has <u>closed down</u>, it has left empty, <u>derelict</u> buildings. Modern industries need <u>more space</u> and don't want to pay for <u>expensive land</u> in city centres. It's hard to attract new business to run-down areas.

<u>High unemployment levels</u> due to the closure of industry can lead to <u>social deprivation</u> in inner cities. Poor quality housing and lack of social amenities have made this problem worse in some cities.

The government has tried to tackle some of these problems with <u>urban renewal schemes</u> aimed at <u>attracting</u> industry to older areas, and <u>encouraging</u> investment in new housing, amenities and employment (see page 96). Also, the '<u>gentrification</u>' of cities means <u>smartening up</u> old existing housing.

Liverpool dockside redevelopment

EXAMPLES

Urban renewal schemes
London Docklands development scheme
Liverpool dockside development scheme
Salford Quays development, Manchester
Bullring Centre, Birmingham

Gentrification
Newcastle, Glasgow and Islington, London have had old inner city housing smartened up.

Retailing Changes Cause City Centre Problems

The <u>doughnut effect</u> occurs when the commercial activity of a city becomes concentrated around the outskirts. <u>Out-of-town shopping centres</u> have become more common, so shops in the CBD have had problems <u>attracting customers</u>. Chain stores have increasingly located in new shopping malls leading to the <u>closure</u> of high street stores.

This leaves a '<u>hollow</u>' or empty area in the middle of the city. The effect began in the USA but is increasingly evident in British cities.

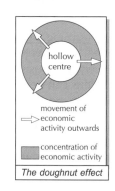

hollow centre

movement of
⇒ economic
activity outwards

concentration of economic activity

The doughnut effect

Urban Problems in LEDCs

Urban areas of LEDCs have a number of problems.

Cities in <u>LEDCs</u> have their own <u>Land Use Patterns</u>

<u>LEDC</u> urban problems come from the difference in layout shown in the diagram opposite. Layout is <u>not the same</u> in all <u>LEDCs</u>, but this model is a good guide.

Notice that the <u>expensive housing</u> is found <u>near</u> the <u>CBD</u> — this is usually modern apartment blocks. The <u>poorer housing</u> is found <u>further away</u>, on the outskirts, making the problem of access to amenities and work even worse.

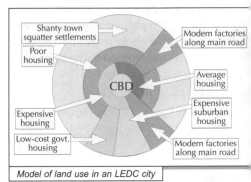

Model of land use in an LEDC city

<u>Spontaneous Settlements</u> are Common to LEDC Cities

Spontaneous settlements are a problem in many LEDC cities. These are settlements built illegally by the <u>very poor</u>, who can't afford proper housing. The settlements are badly built, without <u>basic services</u>. Through time, the inhabitants may manage to improve their shanty town (see page 97).

Shanty town

<u>Overcrowding</u> is a Major Problem in <u>LEDC</u> Cities

<u>Competition for land</u> is intense. High populations and lack of available transport mean people want to live near places where they might find work.

Overcrowding puts <u>pressure on services</u> such as sanitation, health care and housing provision. <u>LEDCs</u> can rarely afford to provide these services for all — this leads to problems with clean water supply and waste disposal, which can create <u>major health risks</u>.

The limited land available means that shanty towns are often <u>built on dangerous ground</u> — e.g. steep hillsides which may collapse in heavy rain, or rubbish tips (a source of livelihood for some). Overcrowding makes this problem worse.

<u>Rural-Urban Migration</u> Worsens <u>LEDC</u> Urban Problems

The <u>rapid rate of migration</u> means it's impossible to know exactly how fast the cities are growing — population numbers are only estimates. This makes <u>planning for growth</u> very difficult.

<u>LEDCs</u> are trying to solve these problems with <u>self-help schemes</u> and government-funded projects, but money is short and the schemes are inadequate for the large numbers involved. While <u>LEDCs</u> have <u>huge debts</u> there is little chance of them being able to solve their urban problems, as they cannot afford the resources they need to sort things out.

Urban Socio-Economic Structures

Where people live in a city affects their quality of life. This page explains why different groups of people live in different parts of cities.

Economic Factors Affect *Where People Live* in Cities

The main thing that determines where people live within urban areas is personal wealth. People with a low income have to live in the less desirable parts of a city, where housing is cheaper. In MEDCs these tend to be inner-city areas, which are likely to be quite run-down, with poor service provision and urban problems like crime, traffic congestion, noise and air pollution.

People with higher incomes are more likely to live in better residential areas, usually towards the edges of cities in MEDCs. Commuting to work is very popular nowadays, so that people can live in the more peaceful, spacious areas outside the noisy and crowded city centre. However, there are also pockets of wealth in inner-cities, where areas have been gentrified.

The Pattern is *Slightly Different* in *LEDCs*

In LEDC cities, the income-based pattern of where people live is the reverse of the MEDC pattern (see diagrams on pages 88 and 90). People with low-incomes usually live on the outskirts of cities — these people are mainly poor migrants who can't afford proper homes within the city centre. They often make up a large proportion of the city population.

Higher income families tend to live in the inner city, next to the CBD, because the highly paid office workers prefer to live close to where they work.

Social Factors also Affect Where People Live

Even though economic factors mainly determine where people live, people who share the same nationality, culture, ethnicity or religion often locate near each other in cities. This means that certain areas take on particular characteristics, depending on the main social group of their residents. For example, shops may sell particular things which are required by the local population, or there may be particular religious services.

Businesses are Spread Across the City Too

Where businesses and services are located also affects where people live.

The CBD is occupied by high-rise buildings and offices for businesses. Governmental and council buildings are also located in the CBD along with the headquarters of many companies. The price of land is high and there is usually little open space, so not many people live in the CBD.

Piccadilly Circus, part of London's CBD

People generally like to live in areas that have good service provision — for example people often try and live within the catchment area of a good school, which pushes house prices up in such areas. Also, some people might choose where they live based on a particular leisure or recreation service, e.g. athletes might want to live near to the stadium where they train.

Case Study

You need to know case studies of the land use patterns in one area, and the urban changes which have happened in another.

Case Study 1: <u>Urban Land Use in Paris, France</u>

Paris has four distinct zones which differ in terms of their land use:

Central Business District (CBD):

- Banking, commercial and shopping areas.

- Some exclusive, high-quality housing.

- Many <u>culturally important</u> buildings such as Notre Dame Cathedral, Pompidou Exhibition Centre and the Louvre museum.

The Louvre in Paris's CBD

Inner zones:

- Some small <u>industries</u> still operate (e.g. the Dior and Chanel fashion houses).

- Some <u>redeveloped housing</u> and smaller <u>shopping</u> zones.

Outer suburbs:

- The population of areas like Versailles and St. Denis is rising because there is very little <u>housing</u> in the inner city.

- There are a number of <u>shopping centres</u> to serve the growing population (e.g. St. Denis).

- There are numerous open-air <u>recreation</u> areas (e.g. the Bois de Boulogne).

Open-air recreation area in Paris

Rural-urban fringe:

- <u>Heavy industries</u> make bulky products on the north-eastern fringe.

- Modern <u>electronic industries</u> are mainly located in the outer suburbs.

- Five new <u>satellite towns</u> have been developed on the fringes to accommodate Paris's growing population.

Case Study 2: <u>Urban Changes in London, UK</u>

London was beginning to suffer problems of urbanisation, so changes have been made to try and improve the quality of life of its people:

- <u>Traffic congestion</u> — <u>traffic jams</u> and <u>congestion</u> have increased, especially during rush hour. Attempts to solve this have included building the M25 <u>ring road</u> to divert traffic around the city, building <u>urban motorways</u> and flyovers, improving <u>public transport</u>, and building new <u>car parks</u>. The most recent scheme is called the '<u>congestion charge</u>' — motorists are charged £5 to enter certain central areas of London, which deters many from driving.

- <u>Pollution</u> — the dense population, combined with <u>traffic</u> and <u>industry</u> has created air, noise, water and visual pollution in the city. Attempted solutions include <u>laws</u> against dumping litter, improved <u>public sanitation</u> (e.g. road sweeping, litter bins), planting more <u>trees</u>, and Clean Air Acts that only allow the use of <u>smokeless fuels</u>.

- <u>Urban decline</u> — There are some areas of London that have declined, becoming run-down and <u>derelict</u> due to business or industry closure. <u>Redevelopment</u> has been successful in zones of previous decline such as King's Cross, Covent Garden and the docklands.

Aerial view of London

Urbanisation

Urbanisation occurs in both MEDCs and LEDCs.
It can create various problems in both rural and urban areas.

Learn the Definition of <u>Urbanisation</u>

Urbanisation is the process by which an <u>increasing proportion</u> of the population become town or city dwellers. The important word is <u>proportion</u> — urbanisation is only occurring if the growth rate of cities is <u>greater</u> than the growth rate of the whole population. Urbanisation is happening on a <u>global scale</u>.
It's also happening on a <u>regional scale</u> in <u>LEDCs</u>.

There are <u>Three Causes</u> of Urbanisation in <u>LEDCs</u>

- <u>Rural-urban migration</u> is occurring on a massive scale due to population pressure and lack of resources in rural areas (see pages 81 and 83). People from rural areas often believe that the standard of living is higher in cities (even though this often turns out not to be the case).

- The <u>infrastructure of cities</u> in <u>LEDCs</u> is expanding faster than in the rural areas, which attracts industrial investment and people looking for work.

- <u>Population increase</u> tends to be faster in urban areas because health care facilities are better, so the death rate is lower. Also, the people moving to cities tend to be <u>younger</u> and so have more children.

Urbanisation has Created <u>Millionaire Cities</u>

<u>Millionaire cities</u> are cities with <u>over a million</u> inhabitants. The world's largest city is <u>Tokyo</u> with an estimated population of <u>28.7 million</u> for the year 2010. (That's the same as half the total UK population.) The only other MEDC city in the top 10 ranking is <u>New York</u>, which has a population of around 17 million.

Aerial view of New York City

Urbanisation Affects <u>Rural</u> and <u>Urban</u> Areas of a Country

It's not just the urban areas that are affected by urbanisation —
the nature of rural areas changes too.

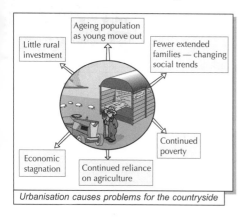

Little rural investment
Ageing population as young move out
Fewer extended families — changing social trends
Economic stagnation
Continued reliance on agriculture
Continued poverty

Urbanisation causes problems for the countryside

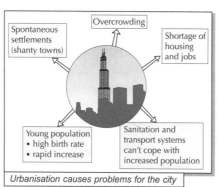

Spontaneous settlements (shanty towns)
Overcrowding
Shortage of housing and jobs
Young population
• high birth rate
• rapid increase
Sanitation and transport systems can't cope with increased population

Urbanisation causes problems for the city

Counter-Urbanisation

Counter-urbanisation is the movement <u>out of cities</u> to the surrounding more rural areas. It has recently been happening in many MEDCs.

There are <u>Six Reasons</u> for <u>Counter-Urbanisation</u>

- <u>Growth in transport</u> and <u>communications</u> mean people no longer have to live where they work. Motorways and increased car ownership have led to <u>commuting</u>. The growth of <u>information technology</u> — faxes, e-mail and video conferencing — means more people can work from home.

- <u>Government policies</u> can encourage movement out of cities, e.g. setting up <u>fast transport links</u> to 'satellite' towns and villages.

- <u>New business parks</u> on out-of-town greenfield sites mean people no longer have to travel to city centres to work and prefer to live on the outskirts of cities to be nearer their work.

- <u>Pollution</u> and <u>traffic congestion</u> in cities encourage people to live in rural areas.

- More people have the <u>money</u> to own <u>second homes</u> in the countryside or <u>move house</u> when they <u>retire</u>.

- <u>House prices</u> in cities have become very high — people are moving out to find cheaper housing.

EXAMPLE
Many of the employees at the large greenfield Cambridge science park live outside Cambridge, in smaller towns like Huntingdon and Ely.

Counter-Urbanisation has a <u>Dramatic Effect</u> on <u>Villages</u>

Village <u>character</u> and <u>function</u> have changed due to the influx of people who work in urban areas. Learn this flow diagram which shows you how.

EXAMPLE
Thurston, near Bury-St-Edmonds in Suffolk, was once a small agricultural village. Now it is home to lots of people who commute to work in London. The rural nature of the village has disappeared, as have the local village shops. House prices have also increased so they're higher than most local people can afford.

> <u>Movement into village</u> of people working in urban areas who want to live in the country.

⬇

> A more <u>affluent population</u> and higher <u>car ownership</u> mean people use services in the city, <u>not</u> local services.

⬇

> An increase in <u>house prices</u> means young people <u>can't afford</u> homes and move away.

⬇

> The village is largely <u>empty</u> during the <u>day</u> — a <u>dormitory village</u>. This leads to a decline in the community spirit.

Quiet dormitory village

⬇

> Local shops and services <u>close down</u> as few people use them. Rural transport provision is also <u>reduced</u> as it is non-economic.

⬇

> Local people without transport have <u>access</u> to fewer <u>amenities</u> — the young and old become <u>isolated</u>.

Planning and the Rural-Urban Fringe

Planning prevents the countryside being eaten up by new buildings. This is called <u>checking urban sprawl</u>, and usually happens at the <u>rural-urban fringe</u> — where the city and the country meet.

Urban Sprawl Leads to Growth of <u>Conurbations</u>

A conurbation's urban sprawl

<u>Urban sprawl</u> occurs when the <u>outward growth</u> of cities is left <u>unchecked</u>, and the city gradually takes up more and more of the surrounding countryside. A <u>conurbation</u> is formed when one city grows so large that it <u>encompasses</u> surrounding towns, forming one huge urban area.

<u>Greenbelts</u> and <u>New Towns</u> — Checking Urban Sprawl

<u>Greenbelts</u> are areas around cities designed to stop urban sprawl. They were set up around most of the UK's large cities in the 1940s, and building is restricted within them. However, some greenbelts have now been released for <u>development</u> due to the need for new housing.

Limiting urban sprawl meant there was a shortage of housing space in the cities, so <u>new towns</u> and <u>expanded towns</u> were built beyond the greenbelt to house the <u>overspill population</u>. This policy has been used in many countries, including LEDCs.

The <u>Rural-Urban Fringe</u> Needs Planning for <u>Leisure</u>

<u>Leisure amenities</u> for urban dwellers are found on the rural-urban fringe because they are easily accessible here, and need more space than can be found in cities.

Amenities such as <u>golf courses</u>, <u>country parks</u> and <u>riding stables</u> have grown in recent years as increased car ownership has meant more people have access to the countryside. <u>Farmers</u> have found that they can make money by expanding into leisure activities such as '<u>pick your own</u>' fruit centres or <u>rare breeds</u> visitor centres which provide a family day out. These facilities have changed the character of the rural-urban fringe.

<u>Planning</u> Has to Get Clever When There's <u>No Room Left</u>

<u>More people</u> means there's a need for <u>more houses</u>.

- <u>Osaka, Japan</u> — Osaka is a very packed (10 000 people per km^2), growing city with tiny houses. When all the flat land was inhabited, houses were built over the sea — this is called <u>land reclamation</u>. The new island provides more <u>spacious</u> housing with facilities and good transport links, <u>easing pressure</u> on Osaka city.

Reclaimed land in Osaka

Liverpool dockland redevelopment

- <u>Liverpool, UK</u> — An increasing <u>demand</u> for housing and government incentives for using <u>brownfield</u> sites has led to the <u>dockside redevelopment</u>, which provides housing and shops in a previously run-down area.

Urban Change

Changes in employment and industry can affect an area dramatically, leading to changes in quality of life for the people that live and work there.

Some Areas have Suffered from <u>Decline</u>

<u>Northern</u> and <u>western</u> parts of Britain have suffered increased <u>unemployment</u> since World War II. This is due to the decline of <u>traditional industries</u> in these areas, which has led to a reduction in available jobs. Traditional industries include coal mining, steelmaking, ship building and textile manufacture.

Traditional industries declined when coal reserves were <u>used up</u>, coal and other products could be <u>cheaply imported</u> and the industries were <u>competing</u> with new, foreign industries, and new products (e.g. plastics competing with steel).

Unemployment leads to a cycle of decline in the community:

Industries closing means that people are out of work and have <u>less money</u>. Less money is then spent on local goods and services, which leads to the decline of the <u>local economy</u> in general. When shops and services close, the area becomes <u>run down</u> and vandalised. There will also be a rise in crime and <u>social problems</u>. This makes it hard to attract <u>new industry</u> to the area.

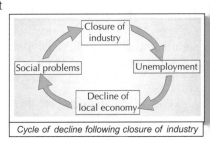
Cycle of decline following closure of industry

EXAMPLES	
Areas that have declined after a manufacturing industry stopped:	
Location in decline	**Industry that has ceased**
Towns in South Wales (e.g. Aberfan)	Coal mining
Sheffield	Steel-making

Other Areas have Experienced <u>Employment Gain</u>

In southern and eastern parts of Britain, there has been an <u>increase</u> in employment opportunities as a result of the growth in <u>industry</u> and <u>population</u>. The growth of <u>hi-tech</u> industries in business parks and industrial estates in the south-east of England has been a major factor in the increase in employment opportunities in the area. The south-east is a good location for industry because of its large <u>market</u> and good <u>communication</u> links with the rest of the country and with Europe.

EXAMPLES	
Areas that have improved due to an increase in new industries:	
Location	**New industry**
M4 corridor, west of London	Hi-tech industries (e.g. computers)
Around Cambridge	Scientific research (e.g. in drugs companies)

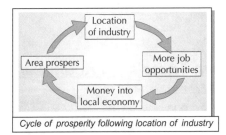
Cycle of prosperity following location of industry

An increase in job opportunities in an area leads to <u>population growth</u> and increased <u>prosperity</u> in the area. With more jobs, there is more money being earned and spent in the local economy, services are likely to increase in number and the <u>quality of life</u> of the locals is likely to be improved.

FACT
Some cities can now be called 'sustainable cities' — these will have some or all of the following:
• recycling of waste
• low pollution
• more use of bikes and other environmentally-friendly transport
• increased use of alternative energy
• less unemployment and housing shortages

Example of Urban Renewal — <u>London Docklands</u>

The London Docklands <u>declined</u> when the ship building industry declined, much of the area becoming derelict. During the 1980s the government decided to improve the <u>status</u> of the area by developing transport, industry, housing and community facilities. This is known as '<u>urban regeneration</u>'.

The <u>Docklands light railway</u> has improved communication links and the transport system. The <u>Canary Wharf</u> high-rise office building has attracted industry and created jobs. The development of <u>housing</u> from old warehouses has attracted city workers and created a community. The area is now deemed to be <u>sustainable</u> because of these factors.

London Docklands

Case Study

You need to know a case study of an LEDC that has been through economic development and has experienced changes in the quality of life of the people.

Case Study: *Economic Development in Brazil*

Brazil's economy improved due to TNCs

Brazil is an LEDC, but it can also be described as a <u>Newly Industrialised Country</u> (NIC) (see page 58). An NIC is one that has seen a significant increase in its secondary and tertiary industries. Traditionally, Brazil mainly had <u>primary sector</u> industry, such as agriculture and forestry. However, over the last twenty years there has been a shift in industrial dominance and <u>secondary</u> and <u>tertiary industries</u> have become <u>dominant</u>.

The main reason for this change has been the location of <u>transnational companies</u> (TNCs). TNCs such as Nike, Pepsi and Reebok have located in Brazil. These TNCs were <u>attracted</u> to Brazil by the cheap labour and land, lax regulations and potential market, but have brought <u>advantages</u> for the country too. They provided jobs, training, improved infrastructure and investment. They also increased international trade and brought in foreign currency, increasing Brazil's wealth.

The location of TNCs started a <u>cycle of economic improvement</u> — the <u>wealth</u> of the people increased, creating a <u>domestic market</u> for consumer goods. Due to this new market, there was an increase in <u>industry</u>, and hence even more <u>jobs</u> and money for the people of Brazil.

Aerial view of Rio de Janeiro, Brazil

WORLD LOCATION

Brazil

BRAZIL LOCATION

Rio de Janeiro
São Paulo

Economic development led to improved <u>quality of life</u>

Economic development means that there is more <u>money</u> available to improve the <u>quality of life</u> of the people. Those who have improved incomes can afford to improve their own quality of life. Additionally, the <u>government</u> has more money available to make improvements for those without improved incomes.

For example, there have been developments to try to improve the favela (shanty town) areas. A government-funded scheme called '<u>Favela Bairro</u>' brought building materials, electricity, water, sewers, roads and social amenities to favela areas in Rio de Janeiro and São Paulo.

This was a <u>self-help</u> scheme, because although the government provided all the materials, the favela residents had to build their own homes. These schemes create a strong <u>community spirit</u> amongst the group.

Quality of life has improved

Revision Summary

This is a big section — take your time on these questions because they're not easy. Don't worry if you can't do them first time round — just keep trying until you can do them all. Go through each one in turn and answer it in full. Treat it as an exam practice — give yourself an hour to do as many as you can.

1) What is the difference between settlement site and settlement situation?

2) Name six different types of settlement sites.

3) Draw the diagram to show the settlement hierarchy.

4) What is an area's sphere of influence?

5) Give examples of high and low order goods.

6) Name six functions used to classify settlements.

7) What three factors lead to the change in function of a settlement over time? Explain each one and give an example.

8) Draw and label the two diagrams to show urban land use in MEDCs.

9) Define these terms:
   a) CBD   b) zone of transition
   c) gentrification   d) dormitory village   e) brownfield site

10) What strategies are being adopted to solve the problem of traffic congestion in MEDC cities?

11) How can the closure of industry lead to inner city problems?

12) What is the doughnut effect? Use a diagram to explain it.

13) Add these labels to the model of an LEDC city below:
    shanty town
    CBD
    expensive housing
    poor housing
    modern factories along main road

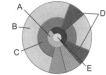

14) What are two negative consequences of overcrowding in LEDC cities?

15) Describe how the following can affect where people live:
    a) economic factors   b) social factors   c) location of business.

16) Describe the patterns of urban land use in Paris.

17) Describe the problems of urbanisation in London, and how people have tried to solve these problems.

18) What is the definition of urbanisation?

19) Describe three causes of urbanisation in LEDCs.

20) What are millionaire cities? Name one MEDC and one LEDC example.

21) What are the problems of urbanisation for the city?

22) What are the problems of urbanisation for the countryside?

23) Describe six causes of counter-urbanisation and how this affects villages.

24) Explain why a) greenbelts and b) new towns were necessary.

25) What is the rural-urban fringe, and what are its characteristics?

26) Describe the planning initiatives in Osaka and Liverpool.

27) Describe Brazil's economic development and its effects.

Sustainable Development

The world's resources are limited and the size of the Earth's population is increasing — so it's not easy to provide everyone on Earth with the resources they need without causing damage to the environment. It's even harder to make sure that people living in the future will have everything they need — but that's what sustainable development is all about.

Energy Resources are <u>Renewable</u> or <u>Non-Renewable</u>

<u>Non-renewable resources</u> take so long to form that they can't be <u>replaced</u> once they run out. These include <u>fossil fuels</u> which have traditionally supplied most of our energy — <u>oil</u>, <u>coal</u> and <u>gas</u>. They are <u>not</u> sustainable and using them is a major source of <u>pollution</u>.

<u>Renewable resources</u> are <u>sustainable</u> resources that won't run out — e.g. <u>water</u>, <u>wind</u>, and the <u>sun</u>. <u>Wood</u> can be renewable too, if <u>replanting</u> is managed well.

Alternative Sources of Energy are being Developed

As <u>fossil fuels</u> begin to run out, <u>alternative</u> energy sources are being adopted:

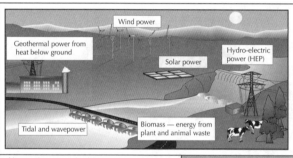

Alternative, sustainable sources of energy

These energy sources use <u>renewable energy</u> so they won't run out, but at the moment there are <u>two</u> big problems with their use:

- Alternative energy sources can't produce as much <u>power</u> as fossil fuel power stations without being <u>gigantic</u>.

- They can be very <u>expensive</u> to set up and maintain.

<u>Conservation</u> and <u>Recycling</u> Provide for the <u>Future</u>

<u>Reducing demand</u> for fossil fuels means they'll <u>last longer</u>, and <u>reduces</u> the harmful <u>effects</u> of using them. <u>Conserving the soil</u> by preventing erosion will provide food for future generations. <u>Recycling</u> metals and paper means using <u>less raw material</u> and <u>cuts energy use</u> too.

Managing Resources is a Balancing Act

Some resources aren't always <u>available</u> where they're most wanted. For example, the fastest-growing demand for <u>water</u> in the UK is in the south-east, but the highest <u>rainfall</u> is in the north and west.

There won't always be enough resources to go round — although LEDCs <u>produce</u> much of the world's resources, most are <u>used</u> by MEDCs. LEDC development means they <u>need more</u> resources.

<u>Multinational companies</u> fear that reduction in consumption will <u>reduce profits</u>.

<u>Research</u> into alternative materials and energy resources is <u>time-consuming</u> and <u>expensive</u>.

EXAMPLES

This table shows roughly how long we have before fossil fuels run out (based on our current rates of consumption):

Fossil fuel	Time left
Oil	50 years
Natural gas	70 years
Coal	250 years

EXAMPLES

Current sources of the world's energy supplies.

Energy source	% of world energy production
Oil	31%
Coal	23%
Natural gas	21%
Biomass	13%
HEP	6%
Nuclear	5.9%
Others	0.1%

Stewardship and Conflict

Stewardship is all about trying to reduce the number of problems
we make for people in the future. But there's a lot of conflict
about how resources and landscapes should be used.

Sustainable Use of Resources Needs Good Stewardship

Stewardship means using resources responsibly so some are left for future
generations and so damage caused is minimal. Stewardship includes:

- Resource conservation: Using resources carefully to slow our consumption
  of them, e.g. making cars and power stations efficient so you use less fuel.

- Resource substitution: Changing resources for more sustainable ones,
  e.g. using recyclable aluminium instead of steel for making cans,
  or using wind power instead of coal.

- Pollution control: Limiting pollution to reduce problems like global warming
  and acid rain.

- Recycling: Re-using resources where possible to reduce the amount
  of waste produced. This is part of resource conservation.

Energy resources should change from non-renewable oil, to sustainable wind

There is Often Conflict Over Land Use

There is a limited amount of habitable land available on Earth. This inevitably leads
to conflicts because people have different ideas about how the land should be used.
For example, in rural places there are often conflicts between farmers and people
who want to use the land for recreation like mountain-bikers. The best solutions to
land use conflicts are the ones which are agreed through compromise, for example

- Making areas into national parks so the land can be managed sustainably
  whilst allowing different user groups to have access.

- Designating areas as game parks in LEDCs to protect the environment,
  provide an income for locals and allow tourists to have access.

- Redeveloping brownfield sites improves the appearance of the areas, provide
  new housing and reduces the need for development on greenfield sites.

Sustainable Development takes Effort and Cooperation

Sustainable development is rarely the easy option — it's often much easier to
carry on with things the way they are rather than changing to be more
environmentally friendly. Sustainability can take place at lots of different levels
from the personal to the global:

- Every person can aim to be sustainable by doing things like
  recycling their waste and trying to cut down car use.

- Decision-makers like local councils and governments have the
  power to bring in policies which support sustainable growth.
  For example some local authorities provide households with separate
  bins for glass and paper to help them organise their recycling.

TIP

Remember that policies
like these rarely make
everyone happy —
there will always be
some winners and
losers. Also remember
that some people /
groups have a lot more
power than others to
get their opinions
considered when plans
are being drawn-up.

EXAMPLES

The Agenda 21 Policy
was agreed at the Rio
Conference in 1992.
The agenda outlines
ways that local
communities can
implement policies
that will contribute to
sustainable
development on a
global scale.

Ordnance Survey Maps

These two pages have everything you need to know about Ordnance Survey maps for the exam — <u>essential</u> if you want to get some easy marks.

Know your **Compass Points**

You've got to know the compass — for giving <u>directions</u>, saying which way a <u>river's flowing</u>, or knowing what they mean if they say 'look at the river in the <u>NW</u> of the map'. Read it <u>out loud</u> to yourself, going <u>clockwise</u>.

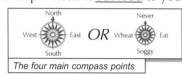

The four main compass points

Use a **Ruler** to Measure **Straight Distances**

To work out the <u>distance</u> between two features use a <u>ruler</u> to measure in cm and then <u>compare</u> it to the scale to work out the distance in km.

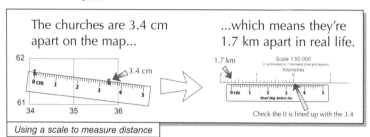

The churches are 3.4 cm apart on the map... ...which means they're 1.7 km apart in real life.

Using a scale to measure distance

EXAM TIP

Using a ruler is the only way to get distances that are accurate — there's no point just trying to guess.

Use **String** to Measure **Winding Distances**

To work out the distance between points along a bendy route (e.g. to find the length of a twisty road or river) lay a <u>piece of string</u> along the route, following all the <u>curves</u>. You can then <u>compare</u> the length of the string with the scale to work out the distance, just like using a ruler for straight distances.

Grid References Tell you Where Something is

There are two kinds of grid reference: four figure grid references and six figure grid references.

Here's how to work out both, for the Post Office on this map.

EXAM TIP

If you're asked to give a grid reference in the <u>exam</u>, always check whether they want a <u>four</u>-figure or a <u>six</u>-figure one.

Four-Figure Grid References:

Find the square you want.
Find the <u>Eastings</u> (across) value for the <u>left</u> side of the square (<u>49</u>).
Find the <u>Northings</u> (up) value for the <u>bottom</u> of the square (<u>70</u>).
Write the numbers together. The grid reference is <u>4970</u>.

Six-Figure Grid References:

Start by working out the <u>basic</u> Eastings and Northings as above.
Then imagine the square's divided into <u>tenths</u>.
Divide it by <u>eye</u> — or even better use your <u>ruler</u>.
The Eastings value is now <u>492</u> (49 and 2 "tenths")
and the Northings is <u>709</u> (70 and 9 "tenths").
The six-figure reference is <u>492709</u>.

Ordnance Survey Maps

This page continues the things you need to know about using OS maps.

Relief is Shown by Contours and Spot Heights

Contours are those orange lines on Ordnance Survey maps.
They're imaginary lines joining points of equal height above sea-level.

If a map has lots of contour lines on it, it's a hilly or mountainous area.
If there are only a few contour lines, it'll be flat, and usually low-lying.

The steeper the slope is, the closer the contours get.
The flatter it is, the more spaced out they are. Look at these examples:

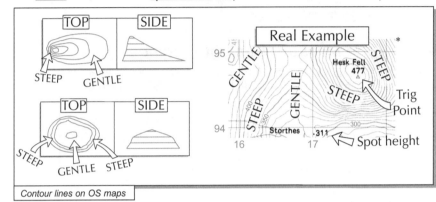

Contour lines on OS maps

A spot height is a dot giving the height of a particular place.
A trigonometrical point (trig point) is a blue triangle plus a
height value, showing the highest point in an area (in metres).

Sketching Maps — do it Carefully

In the exam, they can give you a printed map and tell you to copy part of it
onto an empty grid. Pretty straightforward, but you've got to get it right.

Make sure you read what bit they want you to draw out, and double check.
It might be only part of a lake or a wood, or only one of the roads.

Example: *Q: Sketch the lake and the main roads and rivers on this map*

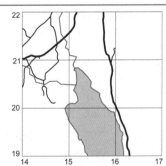

- Get the right shapes in the right place in the squares.
- It's a good idea to measure a few of the important points to
  help you — if you copy a few things over really accurately
  then filling in the other bits will be easier.
- Get the widths of the roads right.
- Draw your sketch in pencil so you can rub it out if it's wrong.

Drawing sketch maps

Human Geography — Plans and Photos

Plans, like maps, show places from above.
And like maps, there are a few <u>tricks</u> you need to learn...

Look at Shapes when you Compare <u>Plans</u> and <u>Photos</u>

The simplest question they could ask you is something like "*Name the place labelled A on the photo*". Names are on the <u>plan</u>, so you've got to work out how the photo <u>matches</u> the plan.

Look for the main <u>features</u> on the <u>photo</u> and find them on the <u>plan</u> — things with an interesting <u>shape</u> like a <u>lake</u>, or big <u>roads</u> and <u>railways</u>.

Example one:

> Q: *Name the place labelled A on the photo.*
>
> A: By the <u>shape</u> of the land, it's either got to be <u>Hope Point</u> or <u>Dead Dog Point</u>.
>
> There isn't a <u>road</u> or <u>building</u> at point A, so it <u>can't</u> be Dead Dog Point — it <u>must</u> be Hope Point.

Photograph of St. James Harbour, 1986

Plan of St. James Harbour, 1984

Comparing photographs and plans

> **EXAM TIP**
>
> If you are asked to look at plans and photos in the exam be aware that they might not be the <u>same way up</u>. Spend a bit of time working out which way up they need to be so you don't get too confused.

The other type of question is when they ask <u>what's changed</u> between the photo and the plan, and <u>why</u>. Look at the shapes to find <u>what's</u> changed, then look at what it's being <u>used for now</u> (check the dates).

Example two:

> Q: *Where has land been reclaimed from the sea? Suggest why.*
>
> A: By the <u>shape</u> of the land, it's got to be <u>Baldy Bay</u> — the sea's further from that building now. It's being used as a car park, so they must have needed more parking.

A typical question about change over time

Plans of <u>Towns</u> and <u>Aerial Photos</u> — Look at the Buildings

When you get a <u>plan</u> in the exam, start by looking at the <u>types of buildings</u> and what's <u>around</u> them.

<u>Small</u> buildings are probably <u>houses</u> or <u>shops</u>.
<u>Bigger</u> buildings are probably <u>factories</u> or <u>schools</u>.

Work out what <u>kind of area</u> it is — lots of <u>car parks</u> and <u>shops</u> mean it's a <u>CBD</u>, <u>houses</u> with <u>gardens</u> mean a <u>residential area</u>, a <u>group of houses</u> surrounded by <u>fields</u> means a <u>village</u>. Always read the <u>labels</u>, they can give you a lot of easy clues.

Example:

> This area has <u>houses</u> with front and back <u>gardens</u>, a <u>park</u>, a <u>school</u> and a <u>college</u>. So it's a <u>residential area</u> — you can tell it's <u>not</u> a CBD and <u>not</u> dense inner-city housing.

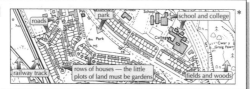

Describing a plan of a town

> **EXAM TIP**
>
> If you get an <u>aerial photo</u> instead of a plan, treat it in exactly the same way as a plan — look for types of buildings and what kind of area it is. You can see the cars and trees which helps, but there won't be any labels.

Describing Maps and Charts

Describing <u>distributions</u> and <u>photos</u> can seem tricky,
but it's pretty easy once you've got the hang of it.

Distribution on *Maps* — *Keep it Simple*

This is an example of the type of question you might get:

Q: *Use the map to describe the distribution of areas with
a population density less than 10 persons per km².*

Questions like this aren't easy — you can <u>see</u>
where those pale yellow patches are, but putting
it into <u>words</u> seems silly. <u>Don't panic</u> — just
write down <u>a description of where things are</u>.

A: The areas with a population density less than
10 persons per km² are distributed in the <u>north of Scotland</u>,
the <u>north</u> and <u>south-west</u> of <u>England</u>, and <u>northern Wales</u>.

A typical question about distribution on maps

Another worked example:

Q: *Use the maps to describe the distribution of National Parks in Spondovia.*

They've given you <u>two maps</u>, which
means they want you to look at them
<u>both</u>. Look at the <u>first map</u> and say <u>where
the blobs are</u>, then look at the <u>second
map</u> and say <u>if there's any link</u> or not:

A: The National Parks are distributed in the <u>south-west</u> and <u>north-east</u>
of Spondovia. They are all located in <u>mountainous</u> areas.

A typical question describing distributions

Describing Photos — *Stick to What They Ask You For*

<u>Double-check</u> what the question's asking. <u>Don't</u> tell them <u>everything</u>
if they <u>only</u> want what you <u>can see</u> from the photo — you <u>won't</u> get
the marks. Look at these two examples for this photo:

The photo shows a 'honeypot'.
List the factors that attract tourists to honeypot locations.
This is asking you to tell them <u>everything</u> you know.

The photo shows a 'honeypot'.
List three factors that would attract tourists to this location.
This is asking you to list <u>only</u> the things you can
<u>see</u> in <u>this photo</u>.

If they're asking you what you can <u>see</u> in the photo, then don't over-complicate
things — stick to what you can <u>see</u> in the photo. For example, if they asked
how <u>people</u> are affecting <u>erosion</u> of cliffs in this photo, then it's by <u>walking</u> on
them (the footpath) — not cars causing acid rain or something.

When you get a photo, look for <u>physical geography clues</u> (what the land's like)
e.g. coastal features and river features, and the <u>human geography clues</u> (what
the land is used for) e.g. the types of buildings, if there are any car parks, if
there are roads or paths, etc.

Use your head — for example if it looks nice and there's a car park,
you can guess there'll be <u>tourism</u>.

Typical questions about describing photographs

Types of Graphs and Charts

Two things you need to be able to do here. Number one: know how to <u>read</u> all of the types of graphs. Number two: know how to <u>fill in</u> all of the types of graphs. It's exactly what you have to do in the <u>exam</u>.

Bar Charts — Draw the Bars <u>Straight</u> and <u>Neat</u>

How to Read Bar Charts

Read along the <u>bottom</u> to find the <u>bar</u> you want.
Read from the <u>top</u> of the bar across to the <u>scale</u>, and read off the number.

Example:

Q: How many tonnes of oil does Russia produce per year?

A: Go up the Russia bar, read across, and it's about 620 on the scale — but the scale's in thousands of tonnes, so the answer is <u>620 000 tonnes</u>.

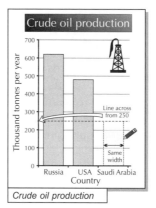

Crude oil production

How to Fill in Bar Charts

First find the number you want on the <u>vertical scale</u>.
With a <u>ruler</u>, trace a line across and draw in a bar of the <u>right size</u>.

Example:

Q: Complete the graph to show that Saudi Arabia produces 250 thousand tonnes of crude oil per year.

A: Find 250 on the scale, trace a line across, then draw the bar in, the <u>same width</u> as the others.

Line Graphs — the Points are Joined by <u>Lines</u>

How to Read Line Graphs

Read along the <u>bottom</u> to find the number you want.
Read up to the line you want, then read across to the <u>vertical scale</u>.

Example:

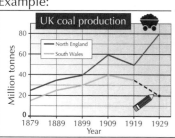

An example question about UK coal production

Q: How much coal did the north of England produce in 1919?

A: Find 1919, go up to the purple line, read across, and it's 50 on the scale. The scale's in millions of tonnes, so the answer is <u>50 million tonnes</u>.

How to Fill in Line Graphs

Find the value you want on the <u>bottom scale</u>.
Go up to get the right value on the <u>vertical scale</u>.
<u>Double-check</u> you're still at the right value from the <u>bottom</u>, then make a <u>mark</u>.
Using a <u>ruler</u>, join the mark to the line.

EXAMPLE:

Q: Complete the graph to show that South Wales produced 20 million tonnes of coal in 1929.

A: Find 1929 on the bottom, then go up to 20 million tonnes and make a mark, then join it to the green line <u>with a ruler</u>.

Types of Graphs and Charts

Pie charts and triangular graphs are both ways of showing <u>percentages</u>.

Pie Charts Show Percentages

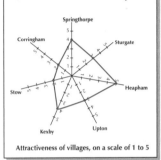
How to Read Pie Charts

Read numbers off a <u>pie chart with a scale</u> like this:

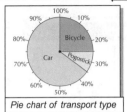

Pie chart of transport type

To work out the % for a wedge, write down where it <u>starts</u> and <u>ends</u>, then <u>subtract</u>.

For example, the 'Car' wedge goes from 35% to 100%: 100 – 35 = <u>65%</u>

They can ask you to <u>estimate</u> the percentage on a pie chart <u>without a scale</u>, but they'll only give you <u>easy</u> ones:

This one's obviously ½ so it's 50%

This is ¼, so it's 25%.

This is ¾, so it's 75%.

Simple pie charts

How to Fill In Pie Charts

With a <u>ruler</u>, draw lines from the <u>centre</u> to <u>0%</u>, and to the number on the <u>outside</u> that you want. Here's how you'd do <u>45%</u>:

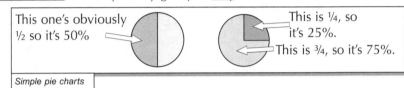

This wedge is 45%.

To do <u>another</u> wedge, you'd have to <u>start</u> from <u>45%</u>. So, if the wedge needed to be, say <u>20%</u>, it would end on 45 + 20 = <u>65%</u>.

How to fill in pie charts

Triangular Graphs Show Percentages too — on *3 Axes*

Triangular graphs look terrible but they're actually fairly <u>easy</u> to use.

How to Read Triangular Graphs
Find the point you want on the graph. <u>Turn the paper</u> so that one set of numbers is the <u>right way up</u>. Follow the lines <u>straight across</u> to that set of numbers, and write it down. Keep turning the paper round for <u>each set</u> of numbers. <u>Double-check</u> that the numbers you've written down add up to 100%.

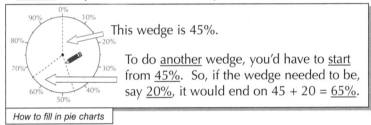

An example of a triangular graph

Example:
The red point shows a population where <u>50%</u> are aged under 30, <u>30%</u> aged 30-6 and <u>20%</u> aged over 60. Double-check they add up to 100%: 50 + 30 + 20 = 100

How to Fill in Triangular Graphs

Start with <u>one set</u> of numbers — <u>turn the paper round</u> until they're the right way u Find the number you want, then draw a <u>faint pencil line</u> straight across. Do the same for the other sets of numbers, <u>turning the paper round</u> each time. Where your three lines <u>meet</u>, draw a <u>dot</u>. <u>Double-check</u> your dot's in the right place.

Types of Graphs and Charts

Two completely different types of <u>map</u> here —
<u>topological</u> maps and <u>isoline</u> maps.

Topological Maps *Show How to Get from Place to Place*

Topological maps like this one show
<u>transport</u> connections. They're often used
to explain <u>rail</u> and <u>underground networks</u>.

It's highly unlikely you'll have to <u>draw</u> a
topological map. If you have to <u>read</u> a
topological map just remember the <u>dots</u>
are <u>places</u>. The <u>lines</u> show <u>routes</u> between
the places. If two lines cross <u>at a dot</u> then
it's a place where you can <u>switch</u> from one
route to another.

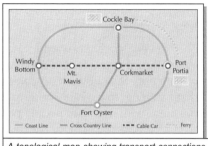

A topological map showing transport connections

> **EXAM TIP**
>
> **If you've got a topological
> map in front of you, make
> sure you check out the
> key — it contains all the
> information you need
> to understand what the
> map is showing.**

Isolines Link Up Places with Something <u>in Common</u>

<u>Isolines</u> are lines on a map <u>linking</u> up all the places where something's the <u>same</u>.

<u>Contour lines</u> are isolines linking up places at the same <u>altitude</u>.

Isobars on a <u>synoptic chart</u> (weather map) link together all the places where the
<u>atmospheric pressure</u> is the same.

Isolines can show different things. They can link up places where things like
<u>average temperature</u>, <u>wind speed</u>, <u>rainfall</u>, or <u>pollution levels</u> are the same.

How to <u>Read</u> an Isoline Map

To read an isoline map you need to find the point you're being asked about.
Then see which isolines the point lies on or between.
You can then estimate the value for the place you're looking at.

It sounds pretty difficult but once you've seen a few examples it gets much easier:
Example:

*Q: Find the average annual rainfall
in a) Port Portia, and b) Mt. Mavis.*

A: Find <u>Port Portia</u> on the map.
It's not on a line so look at the numbers on
the lines <u>either side</u>. They're 200 and 400.
Port Portia's about halfway between,
so the answer's <u>300 mm per year</u>.

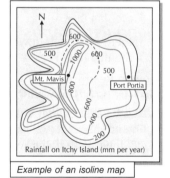

Example of an isoline map

The question about Mt. Mavis is much easier.
It's bang on the line so the answer's
<u>1000 mm per year</u>.

How to <u>Draw</u> an Isoline

Drawing an isoline is like doing a dot-to-dot where
you join up all the dots with the <u>same numbers</u>.

Example:

*Q: Complete on the map the line showing an
average rainfall of 600 mm per year.*

A: Find all the dots marked 600, and the <u>half-finished line</u> with 600 on it.
Draw a neat <u>curvy</u> line joining up the <u>600s</u> and the two ends of the line.
Don't <u>cross</u> any other lines or <u>go past</u> the 500s.
The correct answer is shown as a <u>red dashed line</u> on the map.

> **KEY TERM**
>
> **Isolines are sometimes
> called iso<u>pleths</u>.**

> **EXAM TIP**
>
> **Remember to check the
> units of measurement if
> you're reading figures
> from an isoline graph.**

Types of Graphs and Charts

The last kind of map you need to know about is choropleth maps.
To get the hang of them all you need to do is be able to use a key.
This page also tells you how to describe what a graph shows.

In Exams Choropleth Maps have <u>Hatched Lines</u> and <u>Dots</u>

Instead of using colour coding, the maps in exams usually use <u>cross-hatched lines</u> and <u>dots</u> — because it's cheaper to print in black and white.

They're very straightforward to use, but all those lines can be <u>confusing</u>. When they ask you to talk about all the bits of the map with a <u>certain type of hatching</u>, look at the map carefully and put a <u>big tick</u> on each part with that hatching, to make them all <u>stand out</u>. Look at this example, where all the areas with over 200 people per km² have been ticked.

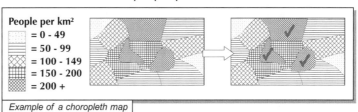

People per km²
= 0 - 49
= 50 - 99
= 100 - 149
= 150 - 200
= 200 +

Example of a choropleth map

When they ask you to <u>complete</u> part of one of the maps,
first use the <u>key</u> to work out what type of shading you need.
Use a <u>ruler</u> to draw in the lines, using the same <u>angle</u> and <u>spacing</u> as in the key.

Describing Graphs — Look for the <u>Important Bits</u>

The phrase '*Describe what is shown by the graph*' is pretty alarming.
It's a <u>nasty looking</u> question, but what they actually want you to <u>do</u> is <u>easy</u>:

The <u>four</u> things to look for:

- Talk about bits where it's <u>going up</u>.

- Talk about where it's <u>going down</u>.

- If there's a <u>peak</u> (highest bit),
  write that down.

- If there's a <u>trough</u> (lowest bit),
  write that down.

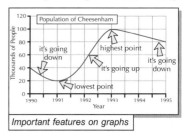

Important features on graphs

Scatter Graphs are About <u>Best Fit Lines</u> and <u>Correlation</u>

With a bit of luck, any scatter graphs will already have a best fit line on them. If not, <u>sketch your own</u> in roughly the right place, then write down what type of <u>correlation</u> there is:

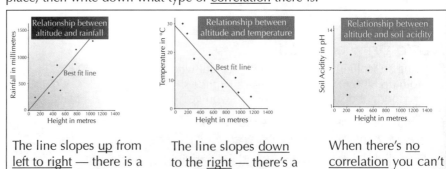

The line slopes <u>up</u> from <u>left to right</u> — there is a '<u>positive correlation</u>'.

The line slopes <u>down</u> to the <u>right</u> — there's a '<u>negative correlation</u>'.

When there's <u>no correlation</u> you can't draw a line of best fit.

The three main types of scatter graph

With this section more than any other, you need to do a lot of <u>practice</u>.
Obviously you have to start by learning the <u>theory</u> of how to deal with maps and
graphs, but the real test is whether you can do it for real in the <u>exam</u>. The best
way to see whether you can do it is to try all these questions. When you've done
them once, go back and learn any bits that you found tricky. Then do it all again.

1) Complete this compass to show all four compass directions:

2) Write down the four-figure and six-figure grid references of all of the
symbols marked on the map that match the key.

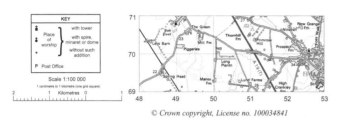

© Crown copyright, License no. 100034841

3) Using the above map, what is the distance, in km, from the post office to
a) Manor Farm, b) Leys Barn, c) the nearest church?

4) Match each contour map with its corresponding shape.

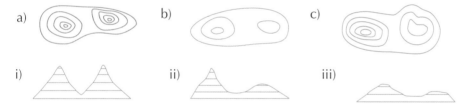

5) a) For each point A to D marked on the map, write down whether the area
is a gentle or steep slope.
b) Give a brief definition of a spot height, and a trig point, and find an
example of each on the map.

© Crown copyright, License no. 100034841

6) From the map above, draw the lake and the outline of the forest (the black
line). First, copy or trace the blank grid above, then measure some of the
important distances to make sure you get things in the right place.

7) What kind of features would you use to work out how a photo matches a
plan of the same area?

8) Describe briefly how you would work out what part of an area had
changed and why, if you had a photo and a plan of the same area with
different dates.

Revision Summary

9)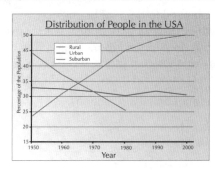

a) What type of graph is this?

b) Complete the graph to show the rural population dropped to 22.5% in 1990 and 19.8% in 2000.

c) What year was the percentage population in urban areas at its lowest?

10)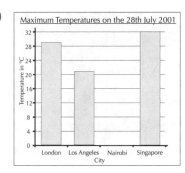

a) What was the maximum temperature in Singapore?

b) Complete the graph to show that the maximum temperature in Nairobi was 16°C.

11)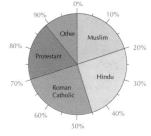

a) What percentage of the population of Surinam is Hindu?

b) Explain in detail how you would draw a pie chart.

12)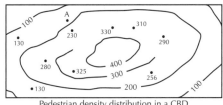

Pedestrian density distribution in a CBD

a) Complete the isoline for a pedestrian density of 300.

b) What is the approximate pedestrian density at point A?

EXAM TIP

There's no denying that question 14 is hard. If you're stuck, remember the 4 things which are important to mention in graph questions:

1) Talk about bits where it's <u>going up</u>.
2) Talk about where it's <u>going down</u>.
3) If there's a <u>peak</u> (highest bit), write that down.
4) If there's a <u>trough</u> (lowest bit), write that down.

13)

Life Expectancy in Southern Africa

Life expectancy in years
☐ No Data
☐ 51-55
▤ 46-50
▨ 41-45
⊞ 36-40
▓ <35

a) What sort of graph is this?

b) Describe the distribution of countries with an average life expectancy of less than 35, or more than 51 years.

14) Describe what the graphs show in questions 9 to 11 and 13.

Key Terms

abrasion — Erosion caused by rocks at the bottom of a glacier, riverbed or sea.

agribusiness — Farms run by large companies like McCain to make profit.

alternative energy — Sources of energy that don't use fossil fuels (e.g. wave power).

appropriate technology — A level of technology which can be maintained by the people using it. Appropriate technology is sustainable, affordable and suitable for the local conditions and people.

arable farm — A farm that grows crops.

arch — An archway in a cliff that has been formed by wave action.

arête — A narrow, two-edged ridge on a glaciated mountain top.

atmospheric cells — The six cells which circulate the World's air masses. They are called the Polar, Hadley and Ferrel cells.

basin — The area drained by one river and all its tributaries.

birth rate — The number of live births per 1000 members of a population, per year.

Central Business District — The middle of a city where land prices are high. It's mostly used for offices, shops and big public buildings.

climate — A term used to describe the typical weather patterns of an area over a long period of time.

Common Agricultural Policy — The policy introduced by the EU to control food production in Europe.

commuters — People who live in one place and travel to work in another.

composite volcano — A volcano made from alternate layers of ash and lava.

confluence — A place where two rivers meet and join together.

convergent margin — A tectonic plate margin where two plates are colliding.

corrie — A semicircular hollow on a mountain caused by a glacier. Sometimes corries are filled by tarns.

counter-urbanisation — Movement of people out of urban areas and into rural areas, a trend which has increased because of an increase in commuting.

death rate — The number of deaths per 1000 people per year.

deforestation — The cutting down of large numbers of trees for wood or access.

delta — An area of land made of sediment which sticks out into the sea at the mouth of a river, where the river splits into a number of smaller streams or rivers.

dependants — People of non-working age who are supported by the economically active members of a population.

desert — A dry area with less than 250 mm of rain annually.

desertification — The process where grassland or woodland is turned into desert due to factors such as soil erosion.

drumlin — An elongated hill of glacial deposits.

ecosystem — The system of energy flows and interactions between all the living and non-living things in one place.

epicentre — The point on the Earth's surface at the centre of an earthquake. It's directly above the focus.

erosion — The wearing away of soil and rock by natural agents like wind and ice.

erratics — 'Foreign' pieces of rock found in glaciated areas. They've been moved, often many miles, by the ice.

eskers — Long, winding ridges of deposited material (many km long) laid down in the channels of streams in and under a glacier.

EU — Abbreviation for the European Union.

evapotranspiration — The loss of water through evaporation (from leaves, lakes, the ground etc.) and the loss of water from plants through transpiration.

flood plain — The area of flat land that surrounds the lower parts of a river. It's made of sediment that has been deposited by flooding.

focus — The point within the Earth's crust where an earthquake starts. It's directly below the epicentre.

fold mountains — Mountains formed by two tectonic plates colliding at a convergent margin.

Key Terms

footloose industry — Industries which don't need to be located near to raw materials. Instead they often locate in pleasant surroundings and near to good communication links.

freeze-thaw weathering — Weathering caused by water freezing and expanding within cracks in rocks.

global warming — The theory that the average global temperature is increasing because of increased levels of carbon dioxide and methane in the atmosphere.

greenbelt — An area of countryside around a town or city where there are building restrictions. Greenbelts are designed to prevent urban sprawl.

Gross National Product — The total value of all goods and services produced by one country in a year, including investments from foreign income. It's often shown per person (capita) to show how the wealth is distributed.

hydrograph — A graph used to show rainfall and the discharge of a river over a period of time.

igneous rock — Rock that is made from solidified magma (e.g. granite).

infant mortality rate — The number of babies that die before they are one year old per 1000 live births.

infrastructure — All of the communication structures and services in an area.

irrigation — The artificial watering of land.

isolines — Lines that join up sites with the same value. For example, contour lines join up points of the same height.

leaching — When rainfall moves through soil washing the soluble minerals down to the lower layers.

LEDC — A Less Economically Developed Country. They're also known as 'developing' countries.

levees — Raised river banks made from coarse river load material that is deposited during flooding.

life expectancy — The average age people can expect to live to, in a particular country (it's often lower for men than women).

kame — A small mound of deposits formed when meltwater streams flow over the snout of a glacier to the flatter ground below.

kettle holes — Hollows in the earth where buried chunks of ice that were deposited by a glacier eventually melted.

longshore drift — The lateral movement of material along a shore in a zig-zag pattern.

metamorphic rock — Rock that has been changed by heat and pressure during volcanic activity o earth movements (e.g. marble).

meander — A bend in a river, usually found in the middle and lower sections.

MEDC — A More Economically Developed Country. Also known as 'developed countries'.

microclimate — The climate in a small area.

moraine — Material that was deposited from a glacier when it melted.

migration — The process where people leave one place to live in another place.

mixed farm — A farm that grows crops and rears animals.

multinationals (MNCs) — Huge companies that have operations in more than one country. They're sometimes called transnationals (TNCs).

multiplier effect — Economic growth in an area caused by one business or industry moving in. It provides a boost to the local economy and attracts other investment.

national park — A protected area of outstanding natural beauty. National parks are popular places for recreation and there are often conflicts over land use.

Newly Industrialised Country (NIC) — A country which has undergone rapid industrialisation since the 1960s. NICs have a lot of foreign investment from MNCs.

non-renewable resources — Resources which will eventually run out because they are being used up at a much faster rate than they are naturally replaced.

pastoral farm — A farm that rears animals.

Key Terms

plucking — A kind of erosion where chunks of rock are pulled from the bedrock by a glacier.

population density — The number of people per square km.

population pyramid — A bar chart used to show the age and sex composition of a population.

precipitation — The deposition of any form of water in the air onto the Earth's surface (e.g. rain, hail and fog).

primary industries — Industries which collect raw materials from the earth. Examples of primary industries are mining and farming.

pull factors — Factors which attract migrants to a place (e.g. good schools and jobs).

push factors — Disadvantages of a place which encourage people to migrate to other areas (e.g. crime and unemployment).

quality of life — How satisfied and happy people are.

quaternary industries — Industries that are involved in research and product development.

renewable resources — Resources like wind power which are continually replaced by nature.

Richter scale — The scale used to measure the strength of earthquakes.

risk — The potential danger that a hazard poses.

roches moutonnées — Small outcrops of resistant rock in a glaciated landscape.

rural-urban fringe — The zone where the city and the countryside meet. It is a popular place for leisure activities.

scree — Pieces of rock that have been broken off a larger piece of rock by freeze-thaw action. Scree slopes form where lots of rocks break off and roll down a hillside.

science park — An attractive, landscaped business park. Hi-tech, footloose industries often locate in science parks.

secondary industries — Industries where the main activity is making products from raw materials (e.g. making crisps from potatoes).

sedimentary rock — Rock which is made when tiny particles of silt and sand deposited on the sea-bed are compressed over millions of years.

shield volcano — A volcano made only from basic (alkaline) lava.

spit — A long, thin ridge of sand that extends from a beach into the sea.

squatter settlements — Illegal settlements of poorly built housing on the outskirts of an LEDC city. They are also known as shanty towns and have other names in some places (e.g. favelas in Brazil).

stewardship — Using resources responsibly so some are left for the future and the damage caused is minimal.

subsistence farming — Farming where the majority of the produce is for consumption by the farmer and his / her family.

suburbs — Housing areas on the outskirts of a town or city.

sustainable development — Development which meets the needs of the present generation without compromising the ability of future generations to meet their own needs.

tectonic plates — The huge plates which make up the Earth's surface. They float on molten rock called the mantle.

tensional margin — A margin where tectonic plates are moving apart from each other.

tertiary industries — Industries which supply services to people or other firms (e.g. nursing).

tombolo — A long beach which joins an island to the mainland (e.g. Chesil Beach).

urbanisation — The increase in the percentage of a population who live in urban areas.

watershed — The boundary between two drainage basins.

weathering — The breakdown of rock by mechanical or chemical processes.

Index

Index

Index